BOOK SALES WON'T MAKE YOU RICH

AUTHOR WEALTH BLUEPRINT

THE REAL TRUTH BEHIND HOW AUTHORS BECOME MILLIONAIRES

NATASA DENMAN

First published by Ultimate World Publishing 2024
Copyright © 2024 Natasa Denman

ISBN
Paperback - 978-1-923255-54-8
Ebook - 978-1-923255-55-5

Natasa Denman has asserted her rights under the Copyright, Designs and Patents Act 1988 to be identified as the author of this work. The information in this book is based on the author's experiences and opinions. The publisher specifically disclaims responsibility for any adverse consequences which may result from use of the information contained herein. Permission to use information has been sought by the author. Any breaches will be rectified in further editions of the book.

All rights reserved. No part of this publication may be reproduced, stored in or introduced into a retrieval system, or transmitted in any form, or by any means (electronic, mechanical, photocopying, recording or otherwise) without the prior written permission of the author. Any person who does any unauthorised act in relation to this publication may be liable to criminal prosecution and civil claims for damages. Enquiries should be made through the publisher.

Cover design: Ultimate World Publishing
Layout and typesetting: Ultimate World Publishing
Editor: Marinda Wilkinson

Ultimate World Publishing
Diamond Creek,
Victoria Australia 3089
www.writeabook.com.au

TESTIMONIALS

Working with Natasa and Stuart as their accountant has been a rewarding journey that showcases the power of collaboration in achieving financial independence.

From the beginning, their goal was to develop their business with the understanding that if they built a significant enough business, it would facilitate their desired financial outcomes. This did take a lot of hard work and effort along with investment and learnings along the journey.

What truly stood out was Natasa and Stuart's ability to run a lean business. They have a deep understanding of the numbers and were always attentive to the key performance indicators that drive success. Their commitment to efficiency and their analytical approach meant that we could fine-tune the business operations to maximise profitability without sacrificing quality.

Moreover, they were eager to learn and open to exploring new investment opportunities. This allowed them to explore implementing strategies that were both safe and growth-oriented. By regularly reviewing their business's financial performance and adjusting their approach, they were able to create a solid foundation for their business while making significant strides in property investment.

Today, Natasa and Stuart enjoy the financial independence they worked so hard to achieve. Their business is thriving, their investments are yielding positive returns, and they continue to maintain a lean, efficient operation. I'm proud to have been a part of their journey and to witness the transformation of their financial mindset. Together, we proved that with the right guidance and a collaborative approach, financial independence is not just a dream but a tangible reality.

David Cassarino, Andresen McCarthy Partners
(Natasa & Stuart's head accountant)

As Natasa and Stuart Denman's accountant for over a decade, I've consistently seen their dedication to financial independence and effective money management, particularly for authors. Every year, their tax return is the first I prepare, and it's clear that they practise what they preach.

Natasa and Stuart bring a wealth of knowledge and experience to the table, making them a trusted authority in their field. I highly recommend Natasa's work to any author looking to take control of their financial future.

Lindsay Roberts (Natasa's accountant)

When Natasa and Stuart asked me to write a few lines about their financial success I jumped at the opportunity. Over the past 10 years working with them as a financial coach and adviser, I have assisted them with financial strategies and have watched them build a very successful portfolio.

They have maintained their personal finances separately from their business and are constantly reviewing and advancing their position. They know their numbers, are disciplined and focused, and are always aware of their overall net worth. They have goals, and consistently monitor progress to ensure they remain on target to meet, or surpass them.

They are not attracted or distracted by new 'shiny things' and believe that unless they can pay for it in cash (and it is not an investment or their home) they cannot 'afford it'. Investment and taxation (together with strategies) go hand in hand with financial success. Good investments with proper strategies helps reduce the amount of tax that they pay on their income and investments.

We regularly review their strategies and investments to ensure they are up to date with the progress and performance of their comprehensive financial plan.

Claudia Rigoni-Brazzale, Sphere Financial Services
(Natasa & Stuart's financial planner/adviser)

I have been working with Natasa and Stuart Denman for more than a decade now on their financial independence goals as their mortgage broker and investment advisor. From the outset they had very clear goals to pay off their home in a timely manner and acquire a number of investment properties that would generate an income to support them and their family ongoing.

They embraced the concept of property diversification with a strong emphasis on cash flow which is a key component to be able to execute the plan. They are two of the most motivated people I have worked with and it has been a real pleasure watching their financial plan come together by building a brilliant, balanced property portfolio.

Garry Harvey, The Property Guy
(Natasa & Stuart's residential mortgage broker)

DISCLAIMER

The advice provided in this book is for informational purposes only. It is not intended to constitute legal or financial advice and should never be used without first consulting with a financial professional to determine what may be best for your individual needs.

The publisher and the author do not make any guarantee or other promise as to any results that may be obtained from using the content of this book. You should never make any investment decisions without first consulting with your own financial advisor and conducting your own research and due diligence.

DEDICATION

The journey to financial independence is not for the light of heart. It takes time, investment in self, action and risk-taking. That is why I dedicate this book to three groups of people:

1. My family and upbringing in Macedonia. I developed my work ethic and saver's mindset from them. I watched multiple businesses grow and provide security for the future amongst my relatives. Being an immigrant at the age of 14 in a country where I did not speak the language also helped me not just survive but thrive.

2. My current family. My husband and children who are my driving motivation and why. I want to ensure they are protected and taken care of not just now but in the future.

3. My financial A Team and Ultimate 48 Hour Author Team! You heard from some of them earlier. Having experts guide you on your financial roadmap to success is invaluable and I cannot thank them enough. My team in the business is like my extended family. I must say they care as much as I do for the business and our authors. I am so grateful to all of them.

CONTENTS

TESTIMONIALS iii

DISCLAIMER vii

DEDICATION ix

INTRODUCTION 1

PART 1: BOOK TO LEVERAGE 3

PART 2: LEVERAGE TO PROFIT 41

PART 3: PROFIT TO FREEDOM 73

PART 4: MILLIONAIRE AUTHORS 103

ABOUT THE AUTHOR 143

THE DENMAN FAMILY COLLECTION OF BOOKS 145

INTRODUCTION

After authoring several books on how to write a book and promote it, I feel this next one was calling me to deliver more than just the strategies I have previously shared. I want to pull the veil on the truth behind how authors become millionaires for life.

This book comes from 14 years of experiencing this for myself, and from watching a percentage of my authors do it for themselves by following a very similar formula. In my experience, it is the development of the 'millionaire mindset' that takes the most time and work. That's why this book is not about specific marketing strategies (those you can learn in *Shut up and Sell Your First Book*). It is about the thinking required to reach the million-dollar (and beyond) level through becoming an author.

Not every author wants to be a millionaire – you may be purely writing your book for legacy intentions and no specific commercial benefit. Perhaps you are wanting to heal, or maybe you just want to give it to your family at Christmas. I've heard all sorts of reasons why people decide to write books. I am happy for all of them and super proud when they achieve their goal of writing and publishing a book. However, if that is you, then this book is not for you.

This is for those who are serious about success in every way imaginable. You don't just want to write a book, you also want to make some serious money and set yourself up for life. You know it will take some sweat equity and investment in time and money. You are willing to put in the work, and want to see it come back to you in infinite ways, paying you back even beyond your physical presence in this world.

Authoring is perceived just like any other creative pursuit. Most authors are poor and broke and have the classic case of a 'garage full of books'. They wonder why, sit with regret and berate themselves that their book content was not good enough to succeed. But this isn't the reason why they never monetised their books. The real reason is this: *they focused on book sales alone to get rich!!!* And when that didn't happen a few months after the book came out, they just moved on to something else. They didn't stay focused, didn't pivot, didn't try new strategies and innovations. They simply put away their writing boots, stored the book in the garage and forgot any of it ever happened ... until the time comes to move house and they realise they have over 500 books sitting there gathering dust and mould.

You can end up one of the lucky ones (one in a million) that does become a millionaire by selling books – but I am not a big fan of those odds. It's like playing the lottery and wishing and hoping you will hit the jackpot this week, this month or this year. It's a long shot. I prefer to improve my odds and aim to win quicker.

I wrote a book a decade ago, *Natasa Denman reveals...1000 Days to a Million Dollar Coaching Business from Home*, where I unpacked how I got to that point. I now am writing the book that unpacks the strategies and mindset behind financial independence via authoring, leverage and investing, so that you and I never have to work a day in our lives to continue to maintain the lifestyle we love.

This book is divided into three parts: 'Book to Leverage', 'Leverage to Profit' and 'Profit to Freedom'. These are the three steps of the Author Wealth Blueprint that you must put into action if you are to live your author millionaire lifestyle.

PART 1

BOOK TO LEVERAGE

As we begin our journey together, we must start at step one. You have your book in hand ... now what? In the pages that lie ahead, you'll learn powerful strategies you can choose to implement that compliment your book content. Each one is explained briefly and some recommendations made of where you can go and find more information. To be honest, I could write a book on each of these separately – for some of them I already have.

Please understand that I have been around for over 14 years leveraging my books and the things I talk about and recommend were not built overnight. They are various strategies I tried at different stages of my business. You don't have to do them all at once. I would even go as far to say that you try one each year and do it well. Master it, refine and lock it in properly within your business model.

Maybe you will decide to purely focus on just one. That is okay as well. Go deep and become the best in the world with that one. You will see which one is my favourite and I do that one 80% of the time and dabble in and out of the others 20% of the time. After all, we know that 80% of our results come from 20% of our efforts. Find yours in the upcoming chapters.

PART 1: BOOK TO LEVERAGE

CHAPTER 1

DEFINE YOUR BOOK'S PURPOSE: LEGACY, LAUNCH OR LEVERAGE

Before we get into any talk of millions, you must first reflect on why you decided to write your book in the first place. Not everyone writes a book to make money. After mentoring over 1000 authors to write multiple books, I have found the reasons people write a book generally fall under three categories: legacy, launch or leverage.

This is mostly focused on non-fiction books as those are the most likely books to provide an opportunity for the author to turn their story or expertise into massive leverage. Fiction, children's books, coffee table books and cookbooks are more challenging to promote and you either need to be a celebrity to sell in large numbers or be that one in a million author that hits the jackpot.

Legacy author

A legacy author is someone that is purely writing their book to tell their life story in the form of a memoir. They generally do not have any intention of commercialising the book in any way. Some of my authors have simply wanted to share their story, leave a legacy for their families, give it as a gift at Christmas to family and friends, or simply experience healing through writing. If that is you, then you don't need to read any further, unless you are curious about what can happen and how you can potentially turn your story into profits.

By the way, I believe that every single book has some kind of legacy within it. No matter the content, the author is leaving a legacy by writing a book.

Launch author

A launch author is someone that wants to start something behind their book. They want to launch a speaking career, create a program or build a business from scratch. I was a launch author 14 years ago when I started this journey and wrote my first book, *The 7 Ultimate Secrets to Weight Loss.* My intention was to write a book so that I can have a 'business card on steroids' to gain credibility and build my weight loss coaching business. I was not known and had no network. I needed something to give me a big boost so that I would get noticed and hired by my ideal clients.

Interestingly, we have seen many times, legacy authors wanting to launch a business or speaking career behind their stories, which when done right can be very lucrative.

Leverage author

A leverage author is someone who has been around for a while, is known as an expert in their own field and who has a wealth of intellectual property and expertise in their heads. This author often may be working one on one with clients and is looking for a way to transition to one to many, or create products online to replace selling their time for money. This author will have the fastest success going from Book to Freedom as they already have an established network and credibility in their own field. They are generally also running their own business and are looking to add more value and variety to what they do.

So where do you sit? Are you a legacy, launch or leverage author? This determines your why that will keep you focused on the journey ahead. Sometimes you may start at legacy and decide to launch something that takes off and before you know it, you are looking for opportunities to leverage. I love seeing that unfold for some of my authors who then get to live the life of their dreams.

CHAPTER 2

NO-ONE CARES ABOUT YOUR STORY

'What? How can you say that? I've lived a very colourful life! I have overcome so much! I have had more things happen to me than others would have over 10 lifetimes. People are always telling me I should write a book.' I have heard this most likely over 10,000 times since I've been in this space.

So, why do I say no-one cares about your story? Well, everyone is worried about number one – themselves. And when they are choosing to buy a book, they are thinking: what's in it for me? (WIIFM) You may have an inspiring story to share, and others can relate to it if they are in a similar situation. This is very powerful. In this chapter, I want to share with you a powerful way to use your story, and a way that is not going to get you anywhere beyond the publishing of your book.

Let's start with the one that gets you nowhere, as I like to finish on a positive note. Writing chronologically about your life from childhood to where you are now is fine; however, some authors make it all about them and all the horrible things that happened in their lives. They portray themselves as a victim and look to prove someone else wrong. They think they hold the power now because it's coming out as a published book. This is okay if you are writing for a healing purpose only.

I've seen this happen so many times in books about domestic violence, sexual abuse, rape, illnesses, losing someone loved, etc. All of these things are very sad, but there is a more powerful way to add value to a reader who is sitting there thinking: what's in it for me?

When we tell our story, it needs to be with a purpose and intention. We don't tell it just for the sake of it. We usually tell stories to make a point, share a way someone else can struggle less through a situation, or use it as a metaphor to inspire others.

We all have many stories from our lifetime that can be shared. Usually, there will be themes in someone's life. Sometimes, there may be five or more major themes. For example, with me, I have the story of being an immigrant as a teenager coming from Macedonia to Australia and assimilating into a new culture. I also have the story of my husband losing a business that pushed me to start this career as a coach and help others write their books. I have my story of being super organised and how all that came about. I have a story of how to travel the world often with a family of five, sometimes six if we include my mum. I have the story about becoming financially independent at the age of 45.

I am not going to share all these stories in this book as they have no relevance to the content. I have chosen one theme for this book, and that is the story of going from Book to Freedom. I know my readers want to know how I did it, and I am here to share the steps, strategies, and know-how that you may or may not choose to replicate for yourself.

When I think about why I buy people's books, this is at the front of my mind: what will this author teach me that I don't know, that will improve the quality of my life or help me solve a particular problem or struggle?

So, when you write your story, what theme will you choose to stick with? If you are a survivor of domestic violence, what did you do to get out, get back on your feet, and set yourself up for independent success? What you went through is still important to share, but even more important is how you were able to help yourself. Others want the shortcuts to your success. Share that, and you will also have the skeleton for your online programs and mentoring you can create later on.

CHAPTER 3

THE MONEY IS IN THE SYSTEM

The rich author creates a SYSTEM from their story, while the poor author just shares their story to satisfy their EGO. The system is the hero, and the ego is the victim. When the rich author thinks about their story, they have the ability to look beyond what has just happened. This author can extract wisdom and practical steps from their experiences that will be helpful to the reader.

Every story has a system built into it. Everything we do, day in and day out on repeat is a system. We just may not have documented it yet. This year in my business, we have become really focused on documenting our systems. That way, when new team members join, they can access exactly how we do what we do, and others can take on the roles of team members when they are away. Ultimately, this is what will make the business saleable for a large sum of money one day. As I said in the beginning, the money is in the system.

People won't pay me for my business success story. The story may inspire them, but it won't help them run the business.

The same goes if you want to be a rich author. Think beyond the story. Ask yourself: what did I do to get to where I am today? What steps did I take to get through the situation, to heal from 'x', or to succeed at 'y'? We don't really learn about systems until much later in life and for some people, never. However, think of the most successful companies in the world and why they are so successful – it's because of a system. Think McDonald's (food, business and real estate system), Apple (electronic device systems), Coca-Cola (the drink is a formula in itself that has been sold for as long as I have been alive), and many more.

Each of these companies has an amazing back story that is interesting to hear, but none of us really care too much about the story. What we are interested in is the taste, the way we feel using their products, and what value they add to our lives.

Start thinking like that if you want to be a rich author. Your readers will learn through your story, but when you pair your story with a system people can follow to achieve their own success, you create a powerful combination. Because guess what? If you help others with your system, they will tell others about you, and that is what will ultimately grow your author platform. There is an old saying that goes like this:

Help enough people achieve their dream, and your dream will be taken care of.

When you create a system, you are also able to leverage it in many different ways that I will discuss in later chapters. That leverage will pave the way to your freedom in due course. The beauty of systems is also that they can be delegated to others, some automated, and ultimately sold for a great profit that sets you up for life.

PART 1: BOOK TO LEVERAGE

CHAPTER 4

EVERYONE FEELS LIKE AN IMPOSTER

I hear you ask: who am I to create a system? I am nothing special. I have nothing to teach. This is not true! This is your buddy Mr Imposter trying his best to wreak havoc in your mind. We all have that voice in our heads, and at times it can be loud. When we are starting something new, it is there all the time, but as time goes on and we grow in experience, we hear it less often. However, it is always there, popping up from time to time to check in on our courage to keep going.

If you listen to interviews with super successful people, you will still hear them talk about their fears, worries and the times they have felt like an imposter. So my advice is just start. Starting, I think, is the hardest and takes the longest. I often tell the new aspiring authors I meet that it takes a bloody long time NOT to write a book!

Even for me writing this book. The idea of what I wanted to share came to me during one of my reading for pleasure sessions the other day. I had a few aha moments and the seed was planted. I opened my phone and wrote a few bullet points. I had the title and tagline already written down. That is what actually came to me first. Then I shared the notes with my husband, and before I knew it, I was writing more bullet points and content ideas as I waited in the car for my daughter at school pick up.

Then I asked a few of my authors (whose stories you will read later in the book) if they would contribute and gave them a deadline. They all said yes within hours, and since I had given them a deadline, all of a sudden I had the same deadline. I sat down and said to myself, I just need to write a couple of chapters and that will make me feel like I have started. So I did. The next day I said, I will write two more chapters, and this morning I woke up an hour earlier naturally, and here I am writing two more chapters.

The book writing engine is in full swing now. The momentum will carry me through to completion, I have no doubt.

Bottom line is that you won't stop feeling like an imposter unless you start. When we are taking action, it feels great, we feel empowered and are in problem-solving mode. You can never fail if you continue to take action. Focusing on helping others always feels amazing. A servant's heart is the main ingredient to putting Mr Imposter to sleep.

You have a genius zone that others would benefit from tapping into. There is always someone out there that is looking for what you have to offer and is a few steps behind where you are now. We are all looking to grow and get ahead in life. No-one likes wasting time, and we are looking for faster, easier and smarter ways to do things. As you have overcome or succeeded at something, embrace that experience and share the steps behind what you did to get there. I am doing that exact thing with this book. When you share authentically, people gravitate towards you even more.

And when Mr Imposter comes to visit again, I learnt this little mantra from one of my early mentors, Kerwin Rae. He said to say this to him: 'I can hear you, you are not me, I am not going to play this game anymore, thank you!'

PART 1: BOOK TO LEVERAGE

CHAPTER 5

THE SLOW LANE

Book sales won't make you rich! One of my least favourite questions I get from aspiring authors is: how many books do I need to sell to make $X? Focusing on book sales alone is a recipe for disappointment and working super hard for tiny returns. I've often had longer conversations with people trying to sell one of my books at $20 versus selling one of my programs at $20,000. That's right, the effort it takes to make large sums of money versus small can be very similar or, I would now even say, it's easier to make larger sales than smaller ones. I will explain how this happens in the next chapter.

Here, let's unpack what a 'slow lane author' does. Maybe you have been stuck in this mindset and have not recognised it yet, or perhaps you are wanting to write a book and don't want to go slow. Getting this right at the front end will get you where you want to go at the back end faster.

The slow lane author mindset: I am going to write a book and, all of a sudden, people will flock to buy it. After all, my story is unlike anyone else's and I want to inspire people through my story. When it comes out, it will just take off and the rest will be history.

The book comes out ... the slow lane author picks up 50–100 sales from their warm network that shows support, and the first few weeks seem like there is great momentum. They are on cloud nine and so proud of themselves for finally writing that book they have been thinking about for 20+ years. They bask in their 15 minutes of fame and then reality strikes.

The crickets start chirping. There is nothing. No-one is talking about the book anymore, and those that bought it have already forgotten it. The slow lane author puts out a few desperate social media posts that add no value to anyone, just buy my book, buy my book, buy my book type of posts, and they sit there scratching their heads wondering why no-one is buying their book. They don't see themselves as business owners and therefore don't end up running their authorship as a business.

After a few months, they decide their book was not good enough, they are not good enough, and forget the whole thing ever happened. So, so, so sad!!! They say they are not good at technology, marketing and sales, and feed their mindset with a self-fulfilling prophecy that in fact turns out to be true. One of my authors that you will hear from later in the book, Francesca Moi, says 'Your life is a 3D printout of your thoughts.' Be careful what you think about yourself, as you just might manifest it into your actual experience.

The slow lane can also be called the 'sloglane' as far as I am concerned. It's a hard, defeating slog in the majority of cases. Once again, yes, there are those one in a million authors that make it to millions of books sold. What I want to teach you is, how to improve your odds. If you end up selling millions of books with the 'expressway', which can also get you there, then you will be rich beyond your wildest dreams.

CHAPTER 6

THE EXPRESSWAY

The mindset here from the get-go is business, business, business. What? But I just wanted to write a book and tell my story ... okay, but if you are selling books, you are making money. If you are making money, you need to declare income and expenses. That is exactly

PART 1: BOOK TO LEVERAGE

what a business is. It's nothing fancier than that. It doesn't matter how small or big it is, the principle is exactly the same.

The expressway to serious money from authorship also comes with a mindset. This mindset is quite different to the slow lane. The expressway author starts out to write a book not to make money from it. They are very much focused on serving an audience that has a particular problem, and they know they will be able to provide a solution. They know the book is not the thing that will make them rich. They are aware there will be more work to do once the book is out. Their vision is much larger and broader. They not only think book, they also think speaking, online courses, other products, running events or retreats, consulting or coaching. They plan to win over high-end clients by giving their book away for free. There is no interest at the front end in profits from the book. This is going to be their 'business card on steroids' and knowingly they invest lots of money to bring out a great quality product. They know the profit lies on the other side of building the leverage machine from the book.

During the publishing process of their book (around three months), they don't just sit there working on the book alone; they pre-launch, share videos, keep people updated and build out irresistible offers that will be launched alongside the book. They don't worry about perfection, they just do their best with what they know at the time and keep moving forward.

The expressway author also doesn't just sit at home behind a laptop. They go out networking, start to nurture relationships with key people of influence and look to help others in whatever way they can. When the book launches, they have a similar boost in initial sales like the slow lane author from their warm network, however they don't really get fazed when those sales slow down. By this stage, they have been asked to speak at someone's event because of the networking they have done prior. They are now more attractive to collaborative partners, who see them as more credible with a book.

At the speaking gigs, they start to pick up clients for coaching and consulting and from a handful of clients they make back the money they invested in writing and publishing the book. Why? Because they didn't just go to the speaking event with a book to sell, they went with options of irresistible offers. Certainly, the book was there for sale at the back of the room, but it doesn't get even a mention. After all, people can see it, it's in the presentation and needs no hard pitch.

This is a big difference in mindsets. The expressway author knows there is consistent work and actions that need to be taken in order for their dreams to become reality. They know building infrastructure behind the book will take time, finessing and skill to learn to market and sell. They are in for the long haul. The fact of the matter is, in the grander scheme of things, it's not even that long. I have seen authors turn their work into millions within three to five years.

Slow laners generally give up somewhere between nine and 12 months. What a waste of time and money! So, which pathway will you choose? When you make your choice, you also must commit that you will learn, take action, follow through and keep trying even when things are not working. The journey is there to challenge you, teach you and make you rich!

CHAPTER 7

FALL IN LOVE WITH SALES & MARKETING YOUR WAY

I know most of you are going to hate me for saying this. I very rarely meet a person who tells me they love sales and marketing. That is also why you rarely meet people of high net worth in life. Their secret is nothing other than mastering the skills of sales and marketing that suit their personality.

This is really important to understand. We are all different. We all have varying strengths and weaknesses and therefore need to find our own style. So, how do you do that? Doing a few different personality assessments can reveal a lot about you. The CliftonStrengths assessment is a good one and lately I've been hearing a lot about Human Design. I love completing such assessments as they either confirm a few things for me that I know or give me ideas of what I should do more or less of.

When you master sales and marketing as a skill, you will never go hungry. These skills are transferable and a lot of people want them. People spend so much money on experts for these skills it's insane.

So why don't you love it? Often, mindset is involved yet again. It is the way you perceive what sales and marketing represent. Perhaps you get a picture in your mind as I talk about it of the slimy car salesman, someone pushy, only out to get people's money or perhaps someone who has to deal with rejection all the time. If I had this picture in my mind, I would hate it too.

How successful and rich people look at it is quite different. They know if they don't market, they stay the best-kept secret. If they don't sell, they don't get to serve. They are aware rejection is part of the game and know that it's not personal. If there isn't a match, they move on to the next opportunity. When magic happens, they know they will be able to help someone which feels amazing and so rewarding. I can't tell you how many people have told me that I have changed their lives when they are holding their first book in hand. Don't you think that feels amazing? That is actually what keeps me going each and every day. To get to the point where someone tells me I have changed their life.

At the end of the day, that is what we need to focus on and picture. So, how do you fall in love with sales and marketing? Right now, you probably don't know too much about it and when we don't know much about something, we are often scared of it. It's outside our comfort zone. But if you start reading books, listening to podcasts and watching videos on the subject, you will become more familiar with the steps, strategies and skills of sales and marketing.

To this day I sharpen my tools when it comes to sales and marketing. The world and human behaviour changes as time passes so what used to work even 10 years ago is not as effective today. Staying on top of trends and learning about these skills consistently is the key to your success. Trust me when I say this: at some point you will switch and actually start to think it's fun and the best thing – so rewarding when it works.

Find your style, pick and practise things you like when you have learnt them and leave out things you don't feel comfortable doing. You can be successful at this no matter your personality type. A quiet reserved person can be just as successful as a loud extroverted person.

CHAPTER 8

DO NOT BUY DONE FOR YOU MARKETING

I mentioned in the previous chapters that many experts provide marketing services that usually come with a hefty price tag. This is all well and good if you already have a clear understanding of what you stand for, who you help, and have your rock-solid offers ready to go. But if you have not mastered sales and marketing on your own, you will be at a huge disadvantage in guiding and instructing someone you hire to help you with it.

When it comes to your story and system, you are the expert. You have the passion, energy and enthusiasm to launch it and put it out into the world. I say until you have made your first 100K on your own, you should not be outsourcing marketing. You can definitely delegate admin, bookkeeping and tasks that take you away from sales and marketing, but please understand that in any business, sales and marketing should be the final two departments that you outsource or delegate.

Just take notice of people you follow online or maybe some you have learnt from. Generally, there is a face to the business that you are familiar with. This person does videos, sends you emails, you regularly see them post on social media, they may run events or you see them speaking. This is all sales and marketing. I do all this in my business, and I have done so for the past 14 years. People come to me out of nowhere nowadays and often the comments go like this: I have been following you for a while now, I have watched so many of your videos or been on your email list for years. Then they sign up to work with me. Easy, hey?

Not quite. I committed from day one of this journey to be visible, to add value, and share my journey over the years, not just sporadically but consistently and unashamedly. Those that like me, love me, and those that don't, I wish them well. They will find their match with someone else.

Find a company that will teach you sales and marketing when you write your book. When I created Ultimate 48 Hour Author, it was never just about helping people write and publish their first books. It was always so that they see the potential that I saw. How lucrative leveraging a book can be and how far you can go with it if you follow the process that I outline in this book.

I love teaching my authors sales and marketing as I know that is what will get them a return on investment of their time and money. We do six full-day masterclasses throughout the year on the various topics in this book, weekly workshops and the coaching couch with Nat every two weeks. Remember, you don't know what you don't know, and when you know it, you hold the power to do what you please with it.

So please, only get done-for-you marketing once you are the expert in your own marketing and sales. Otherwise, you may as well flush your money down the toilet, as it is not guaranteed. If you don't know how to guide it, you will not get results.

CHAPTER 9

PRODUCT POWER

When you write a book, you become a producer. A producer of content that can be leveraged in many different ways. This is the secret to great riches from your authoring journey. Your authoring journey doesn't stop when the book comes out. It actually starts, and in a big way, if you do all the things I am about to teach you.

PART 1: BOOK TO LEVERAGE

The first thing you can think about is the creation of other products that complement your book. They can be online or physical. We will talk about an online course in a later chapter, so here I want to cover physical ones.

You would be familiar with the book *Elf on the Shelf.* Now a Christmastime staple for families with young children, it was popularised by the little elf that comes with the book. Can you believe this book came out just 14 years ago? Now a global phenomenon, most don't realise that it started with a book. The book teaches the system, and the elf is the product that comes along with it. It is the elf that has become the hero, not just the book. One powerful product leverage. Last year, I had to buy another one because my kids wanted the girl elf. If you want the original, you have to buy the boxed set that contains the elf.

Later in the book, you will hear from one of my authors who has created branded jewellery, protein powder, T-shirts and branded planners to aid the brand she has built from publishing now three books. Even writing multiple books is a smart idea for leverage. You can package them as a trilogy and sell way more than you can with just one.

I have created many products over the years. My physical ones include my 14 books, two planners (*Ultimate Business Planner* and *Ultimate First Time Author Planner*), and a ton of what I will be speaking of in the remaining chapters.

It is really nice for someone to have something tangible from you when they engage with you or your book. The perceived value skyrockets, and they feel a greater sense of connection to you and what they are learning. Products also help greatly to get your brand out there. People hold on to books and products in their physical space for a lot longer than some ebook that was downloaded and then lost in cyberspace or in most people's overcrowded computers and inboxes.

Creating physical products is not easy or cheap. Just like self-publishing a great quality book isn't easy or cheap. You do need to calculate your costs of production, postage and distribution before you jump into it. But just like print on demand is available for books, you can find many options for creating smaller quantities of your products to start with. If you intend on speaking, running events and doing things where you are physically there with people, physical products will likely sell because people have gotten to know you, like you, and trust you a lot faster. The sale of products at events can easily cover the costs of running those events and travelling to them.

Products are just the starting point that can turn your intangible system into something tangible for the benefit of your readers or fans. Get creative, or you can use AI nowadays to brainstorm ideas on what you could create. Just type into the AI tool what your book and system are about, and it will spit out lots of ideas you can consider moving forward with. I love using AI for brainstorming.

CHAPTER 10

WRITE MORE THAN ONE BOOK

I touched on this in the previous chapter, and here I want to delve deeper. As I mentioned, once you've written your first book, you become a producer. Similarly, when someone starts a podcast, they don't just record a single episode. Over time, you learn more, you grow and sharing this knowledge is incredibly powerful. This book is a perfect example of that for me. It's my 15th book in 14 years. Why? Because each year, I put into action everything I learn, do and implement. I hit particular milestones in my life and career that I couldn't have written about in hindsight any earlier.

The reason this book has come about is because I reached the financially independent milestone when I turned 45. I'm now looking back and sharing what worked, the mindset I needed to develop, and the steps I took to get to where I am today. I couldn't have written this five or 10 years ago. I firmly believe that to reach the success you envision for yourself, you must be authentic and share what is true to you so it can help others.

Writing more than one book also helps you become a better writer and speaker. The more you write, the greater level of expression you reach. You also refine your speaking skills and can express yourself with clarity and ease in front of audiences who truly understand what you're saying. You know this when they come to you afterwards to share how inspired they are or quote something you said. So, if you want to be a great speaker, write more.

As you write more books, you produce more. People who continue producing make the money. They become thought leaders that others start to follow, share and remember. The more you write and produce, the more you stay top of mind with people in this world. We are flooded with so much information from email, social media and TV, and those who stay in touch with us and whom we start to recognise are the ones who will be remembered. If you only write one book and never talk about it again, or at the very least start producing some content around the system you've shared, people will forget.

In life, we need to keep launching and re-launching what we do and what we stand for. Often, people think one book launch is it. That part is done, and my book is launched. But if you look deeper, the reality is the most successful authors have multiple launches in multiple cities over a period of six to 12 months, touring around sharing their work.

I was listening to a podcast yesterday, and the presenter shared that she launched one of her first books in various cities at local cinemas to cut down on costs and have a great stage with AV and ample parking on site. Clever idea, but best of all, she did this in many cities and locations for maximum impact and exposure. This person has now also written multiple books herself.

Think of people you admire and look up to, and you will notice they all have something in common. They have either written multiple books or consistently produce new content in the form of videos, podcasts, social media posts and emails. They are the rich authors.

CHAPTER 11

HOW DO YOU SERVE?

As mentioned earlier, no-one cares about your story – but they are keen to see what's in it for them. As we go through life, we experience situations and learn through setbacks, which gift us wisdom and hindsight so that we know better moving forward. What would you advise the past version of yourself? The books we write are often not for other people, but for the past versions of ourselves. It just happens that there are people where we once were, searching for answers and an easier way forward. It is your system they are after. How did you get from A to B, overcome C, or achieve D?

It is time to think about how you will serve these people. After all, I am sure you proclaimed that you wanted to make a difference in the world and help others when you started your authoring journey.

One of the easiest and fastest ways to get things off the ground financially is to create some services that you can offer people. Usually, these are in the form of coaching or consulting within the area you have written on.

When I started out purely as a life coach, 14 years ago, we were told to come up with coaching packages we could offer when someone was interested in working with us. I put together three-, six- and 12-month packages, and this is what I would show those that came to have a session with me. When I wrote my first book, *The 7 Ultimate Secrets to Weight Loss*, I just customised the packages to be around weight loss coaching.

As my credibility grew and I got a few speaking gigs at various health-related businesses that were complimentary to me but not in competition with me, I would offer the attendees an opportunity to have a couple of low-cost sessions with me packaged with the book. More than 70% of people from those opportunities took up my low-cost offer, and even though I was losing money at the front and spending a lot of time doing low-cost coaching sessions, more than 95% of those who tried my coaching stayed on as fully paying clients after the first couple of sessions. I was fully booked in under six months, and that is how I first hit six figures in revenue with my business. I was highly profitable, but I was selling my time for money, which ultimately was not scalable.

Nevertheless, it was through doing one-on-one that I learnt so much about what worked, what didn't, and how to continue to refine my system further, which enabled me to later license it and sell it one-to-many for others to do the same type of coaching with their own clients.

So, how can you package up some services that allow you to help people? Think about bundling together tangible and intangible inclusions and how you can add as much value as possible, turning it into a 'no-brainer' offer. If you want to know more about this, simply search on YouTube 'Natasa Denman packaging and bundling' and you will find a couple of public videos where I teach this. If you develop this skill right, you can have so much fun with it. I package and bundle everything now – my events, VIP upgrades, retreats, online portal and membership. I will share in the upcoming chapters some ideas of how you can do this for yourself too.

For now, if you are just starting out, or your book has just come out, devote some time to serving others one-on-one. Get some testimonials and experience under your belt that will help you reach the next level with more ease and confidence.

CHAPTER 12

ONLINE COURSE

Everyone is looking for passive income. We all want to work less and enjoy more of our lives doing things we love, when we want, how we want, and with people we love spending time with. So, if you have written a book and have a system behind your story, creating an online course should really be on your next 'to-do' list to leverage your content. After all, not everyone is going to be ready to work with you one-on-one or be able to afford that level of service.

Creating an online course gives you another option to offer and support your ideal clients. Online courses can be free, low-cost or high-end. What you create will be up to you, but in the main, I strongly recommend learning how to build out and launch an online course, no matter the size or price you plan to put on it. The world is learning online every single day, and the speed and efficiency that

PART 1: BOOK TO LEVERAGE

people experience in the privacy of their own homes with online courses is amazing.

As you are a thought leader now, you must build out your suite of products and services if you are to become a rich author. I created my online course eight years ago, and as it's my signature Ultimate 48 Hour Author program, I sell it at $2000. A few years ago, we decided to turn it into what we now call the Online Portal, packaging it up with a few other value-adding items to turn it into a huge bonus. We added a second online course I did before my signature one called Bums on Seats, membership in my private Facebook group, and access to all my recorded training I have done over the years. Literally, hundreds of hours of content on leveraging a book and the business behind the book.

We have sold this course over and over in the past eight years. It is not our core offering but a wonderful way to down-sell to a more affordable level for some people or even sweeten the deal on some of our high-end programs by offering it as a bonus. It has generated 500K in revenue just by being available passively. I would say that is a pretty great return on my investment of time eight years ago. As I knew my stuff really well, all it took me was three days: one day planning my modules and templates, one day filming 12 x 30-minute videos, and one day uploading and setting it up online so that others can start taking it.

If you have never done something like this, my recommendation is to start small and work your way up to your signature program. Once again, if you skipped the step of working with clients one-on-one, this is what I would recommend you go back to and gain experience of what they really want and what they respond to. I had been running my program for more than three years when I decided to create the online course to complement my other offers.

When you do create it, make sure to also package and bundle it with other supportive inclusions that will help your clients get to success easier and faster. As you grow and create more content, add more value to your package.

CHAPTER 13

SPEAKING PLATFORM

Having worked with almost a thousand first time authors, I must say one of the main things they would like to do when their books come out or even before they come out is to speak about their story and share their message with the masses. I am very happy when I hear this as I know that they will sell the most books when in front of people but also they will be able to offer more than books if they have set up their other products and services right to complement their book.

However, the reality is that very few end up doing it. Once again, just because you have written a book, people won't come seeking you out for speaking opportunities. You must have a process to find them and book them in. Speaking is one of the best ways to leverage your way to millions. The best bit is that it doesn't even have to be paid speaking. Both myself, and my authors that have done this work, are proof it can be done and there is a process to be followed in order to succeed.

So what do you need to do to start getting speaking gigs? I will give you the brief version of the main ingredients here. I encourage you to read further books written on this topic or attend seminars and training to learn the nuances behind these steps.

PART 1: BOOK TO LEVERAGE

Here are the ingredients:

1. Come up with three keynote topics related to your content that you can offer event organisers. Make sure they also have three key takeaways listeners will walk away with when they hear you speak on each topic.
2. Design a speaker bio that includes the topics and a 150-word introduction of who you are. This is what event organisers will use to introduce you. Make sure you add your book, photo of you and any credibility-building images to the design. You can hire someone on Fiverr to design it for you or do it yourself for free on Canva.
3. Start attending networking events in your city and look to connect and build relationships with key people of influence (the event organisers and other speakers). Do not ask for speaking gigs the first time you meet people, but do have your speaker bio handy in hard copy and saved on your computer as a PDF in case there is a speaker call out online.
4. Look out for speaker call outs on social media – if there is one, don't be like everyone else that just comments on the post with 100s of other people. Take some time to come up with a personalised message that you will privately send to the person that is looking for speakers and alongside it, attach you speaker bio. This sets you apart, as 95% of people that say they want to speak do not have a speaker bio.
5. Google 'speaker callout' alongside the current year and you can find lots of conferences that are looking for presenters. You will need to go through an application process and I recommend you take the time to do this properly. Save all your answers in a word document so that in future you can copy and paste those answers into similar applications. The work is done once but

can be used multiple times with just small adjustments according to the requirements of the next company.
6. When you do get gigs, often you may get approached by other event organisers to speak at their event if you did a great job. Always book in the next opportunity then and there so it happens.
7. Always send any requirements to event organisers immediately (within 24 hours) so that you look reliable, prompt and excited at presenting for them.
8. Follow-up after your speaking gig to say thank you to the organiser and let them know if they found it helpful and valuable that you would be happy to return again at a future date.
9. Share photos on social media of you speaking and in front of groups of people and when you get a good one, be sure to add it to your speaker bio design. When people see you speaking they may reach out and ask you to speak for them. Don't forget online is huge in today's world, so make sure you are also saying 'yes' to those opportunities too. This is your chance to go national and international.
10. Make sure you go into events with your speaker kit. For an author, this would be: pull up banner, branded tablecloth for the table where your books will be sold, books, business cards, a device that will have a presenter timer so you stick to time and your offer sheet.

The final point is really important. Once again, I have seen authors get gigs and then make no money because they did not tell the audience what the next step was. Sometimes they didn't even tell them the book was available for sale. Make sure that you check with the event organiser having an offer is okay and share with them what you plan to have. Always give them a lucky door prize in the form of your book or one of your offers. If you can't have an offer then the door prize lets people know what you have and they can chat to you after.

I am going to leave this here as I could write a whole book it if I keep going. Speaking is a high touch strategy that builds rapid trust with people and therefore brings super quick results in terms of money and conversion.

CHAPTER 14

MEMBERSHIP

Another scalable asset you can build into your business is setting up a membership model for your clients. Having recurring revenue that can be scaled in a massive way is very attractive. This is also a great option for those clients that can't afford to work with you in the most intimate way that is priced at the high end. It is not passive income, however, you can be serving thousands and only have to work a few hours per week.

Memberships can be used at the front end of your business model or at the back end. In this chapter I am briefly going to share the three key challenges to consider when you are thinking of designing your membership. For the rest of the in-depth nuances, I recommend checking out Stu McLaren who has a great program called 'The Membership Experience'. He goes into amazing detail and shares many strategies on how to be truly successful with memberships.

My journey into memberships began a bit over two years ago. I launched the Ultimate Momentum Membership for my back-end authors and a year later I rebranded it to the Book Accelerator Membership that serves both front end (10%) and back-end authors (90%).

Start with packaging and bundling amazing value so that your membership seems like a steal when you present it to someone. Visit www.writeabook.com.au and click on our membership page to check out how we have done it. Run a founding members' launch, limited to a certain period of time or for a certain amount of people. I gave my first 10 founding members a special entry price point we have never given anyone since.

The MOST IMPORTANT thing in your offer needs to be what I now call the STICKY BONUS. One of the biggest challenge with memberships is client retention. How do you get clients to continue paying their monthly fee without cancelling out just because they are not using the membership regularly? You can lock them into a 12-monthly agreement, however I am not a big fan of this. I also don't like to have to explain agreement obligations to clients that want to pull out. It's really awkward and then it would make me feel like they are stuck paying for something they don't want.

Instead, think about a STICKY BONUS. In our membership, I say there are no lock-in contracts, and we have 30 days no questions asked money back guarantee so people can try it at no risk. The best bit is, when you have been a member for 24 months consecutively you get a standard book publishing package fully paid off. So not only do they get four types of weekly workshops/support calls, archives of past workshop topics, a private community and access to me, they also end up getting a publishing package after 24 months. That is like getting two things for the price of one. The membership at the time of writing this book is $367 per month making it $8808 over 24 months. A publishing package is $6695 – so in fact they pretty much are getting the bonus for free.

For my in-house authors, this has enabled them to write multiple books without having to come up which a chunk of money every two years. I am seeing them now roll over into the next 24 months as they know there will be a new book they will have ready by then. For my new authors, it's a way into our system and community without the 20K price tag.

This is not my main offer, yet it generates currently 30K of recurring monthly revenue for the business with its 100 members. Could I scale this further? Absolutely. I even added another tier to it recently at $497 a month. This includes attendance of our signature Ultimate 48 Hour Author retreat after 12 months and the publishing package at 24 months.

This keeps my members in for the long haul. Even if they are not using the weekly support calls and workshops, they know at the very least they are paying down their next book publishing package.

I got this idea from the company that built my website. Building an amazing website that brings results can be really expensive, sometimes well over 10K. So, when I was considering working with them they presented me with a 'no brainer' offer. An initial set up fee of $1500 and then $197 a month ongoing for their Concierge VIP support. The best bit about it? After 24 months at this level, I would get a full website refresh at no cost. The look, feel and functionality of websites changes over the years and our branding may start to feel outdated, so having a refresh really keeps you looking sleek and current.

We took up this bonus just recently. I am so happy as I get a brand-new looking website that incorporates my updated branding colours and fonts, yet I don't have to come up with any extra funds.

Take these two examples and come up with your STICKY BONUS. From there work backwards to set up your membership offer. Will members still pull out? Of course, that is the nature of memberships

– but I bet your rate of cancellations will be minimal in comparison to not having a STICKY BONUS. Whenever someone tries to cancel with us, I have a template email reminding them of the bonus they are working towards and 9 out of 10 times they decide to keep going because they don't want to miss out on that bonus.

CHAPTER 15

LICENSING

I want to remind you – the money is in the system. One of the best ways to impact millions with your system is to be able to clone yourself. As that is not scientifically possible yet, another way is to license your system and train others to do what you do. Most people lack the confidence and knowhow to create a system of their own, so they would be more than happy to buy into someone else's already established framework for success.

Think McDonalds and the thousands of other franchise models, multi-level marketing companies, personality profiling systems, car hire companies, Airbnb, Uber, etc. They are everywhere! Someone was courageous enough to try a system and do the work to promote it and now millions of people are using it and/or benefiting from it. Why can't you be that innovator? You don't need to go as big as some of the companies I have mentioned, but you never know unless you give it a go.

My first experience of this was when I ran out of time to take on any more one-to-one weight loss coaching clients. My mentor at the time suggested that I always document what I do with my clients, from onboarding to the coaching and everything in between. I started doing this in my second year in business and by the end of six months I had created all my systems. Then the idea occurred to me, now that I have this I could sell it to others to use that did not have any system at all.

I started out as a generic life coach with no system, so I knew other new coaches would be feeling the way I was. They would be able to have a couple of sessions with clients but then they would run out of things to say. Not only that, generic life coaching is really hard to sell. My system was all about solving a problem which was weight loss and it was further niched into 'Lose the Last 10 Kilos'.

I once again pulled out my packaging and bundling skills, built out the training manuals, hired a lawyer to help me with the licensing agreement and went to the people that had said to me 'I want to do what you are doing.' I sold the first seven licenses easily. This was my first experience of moving from one-to-one income to one-to-many. This was also the strategy that got my husband to quit his day job two and a half years from the time I started. We became totally self-reliant purely on our business revenue as a family and are going strong almost 12 years later.

For me, the licensing didn't continue for a long time (we did it for around 18 months) as I pivoted to our now Ultimate 48 Hour Author model. However, we sold around 40 licenses during that time which is also how we hit our multi six-figure level with the business.

Lately I have been writing the systems for Ultimate 48 Hour Author with my full team as I know this is either my exit strategy for the day I may decide to sell the business or I may take it to a licensing opportunity if I choose to. With systems, the opportunities and leverage is massive. Start today working on yours one or two hours a week and you will be amazed how much you will end up creating in three to six months' time. Your clients will be grateful for how organised everything is and you will have more options around your business and your offers.

CHAPTER 16

GROUP MASTERMINDS

The leader in any field, always benefits the most. The more responsibility you take, the greater rewards you will get. Masterminds have been known to provide massive value to their participants. So why not start your own? This may not be a huge revenue stream for your business, but it can definitely be at least a six figure one. The best masterminds are around 12–15 participants. There are free masterminds and paid ones.

If you are going to join one, I recommend that you find a paid one – and if you are going to create one, I recommend that it ends up being a paid one. The reason for this is that when people pay, they also pay attention and commit to attending the meetings and helping each other. They are keen to get return on investment for their time and money so the value they bring and give is ten-fold to a free mastermind.

There are great books out there on how to go about creating a mastermind successfully. Unlike a membership, I suggest you have an annual fee for this so that people don't come and go, as this is very disrupting and annoying for the other members in the group.

You want to look for people at varying levels of success and different types of business models. A mix of younger and older members, male and female, and people from different cultures is ideal. The more varied, the better, as masterminding is all about seeing challenges from different perspectives and viewpoints. What you see is very different to those that are not in your industry/niche and those that are not emotionally attached to your problem.

My experience of a group mastermind was when I created one that I ran at my home over a two-year period. This was slightly different to what I have described as I was also the mentor, teacher and facilitator of each monthly meeting. I charged 15K for the 12 months. This gave the members one day per month attendance at my home where we delved deep into a topic for half the day and the second half we went to a different part of our home and masterminded for the second half on each person's business. It was really powerful and useful for all. The ideas that flowed and were shared could not have just come from me. The members helped one another and I just facilitated most of the time. After the meetings, they went away for the month with plenty of things to put into practice, and they would come back next month with a report of what happened.

We also developed really deep relationships over the year, so collaboration was big between all of us, and we shared a huge sense of comradery. When we think about masterminds, the return on investment comes from ideas generated to further grow your business. If you are not confident to start your own yet, I suggest being part of one for a couple of years, so you can learn from it. You can then create your own model based on what you have learnt, experienced and read about them. You will never regret it. Business can feel like a lonely journey especially if it's just you, so find your team in the form of a group mastermind.

CHAPTER 17

EVENTS AND RETREATS

Woo hoo!!! My favourite strategy to make millions! It's not for everyone, but it is hands down my absolute favourite. I've been doing it consistently since I started in business 14 years ago. Why you ask? Because unlike speaking, you are the boss of your stage – you can do and sell anything you like. Unlike an online course or a membership (which is mostly online), you build rapport and relationship with real people in real life. Connections are made much faster with people face to face, resulting in more rapid conversions and sales from your events.

Even during the pandemic, this pivoted easily to an event and retreat online model that made those years our most successful to date. Events and retreats are an experience that your clients will never forget if you do an amazing job and facilitate transformation for them. For an in-depth look at running events and retreats successfully, check out my *Bums on Seats* and *Fully Booked Retreats* books. They go into so much detail on turning events and retreats into a multimillion-dollar strategy.

It's not easy, but so rewarding and so profitable when done right. If you are an extrovert like myself, this is my number one recommendation for you to try. This platform can help you sell everything in your arsenal – books, online course, one-to-one consulting/coaching, the high-end retreats, membership. Everything is possible. All you need is to come up with your million-dollar event presentation and a focused rock solid offer. DO NOT offer to sell all of the things I listed. You can certainly down-sell and cross-sell to the other things but DO NOT offer multiple things at your event. Less is more in this case.

My signature half-day seminar has been running over 11 years now. If you want to check out my multimillion-dollar formula, come along for FREE to the next online or face to face one. Just visit www.writeabook.com.au and you can find links to the next one that is happening. I run it around 40 times a year, which means to date we are getting close to having run it 450 times LIVE. Yes live, not pre-recorded and rolled out as an evergreen webinar – LIVE! It takes a lot more effort, however the rapport, connection and results it brings is totally worth it.

Over the years we have tweaked and adjusted the content to suit the changes in technology, environment and our growth, but the foundational premise of it has never changed. One single seminar run 450 times filling so far 50 high-end retreats resulting in over 15M in sales. You may be thinking – are you not sick and tired of doing the same thing over and over? Sometimes I get tired and yes I feel a bit over it but 90% of the time I absolutely love it. I love it because my participants are always different, the books they are writing are different and that is what keeps it varied and interesting. And how can you be sick of people saying you have changed their lives, as your teaching has given them the skills and confidence to take the next steps? NEVER!

So how do you arrive at your winning million-dollar event formula? It's not rocket science. Clarity comes from ACTION! The more action you take and the more event topics you try, the more you will understand where people see value from what you present. The sad things is most will try running two or three events max and then give up, due to lack of bums on seats or an inability to close anyone on their offer. See the thing is, after two or three events you most likely are not even a good speaker yet. You still have your training wheels on and you only get the size of groups that you can handle.

I ran and spoke at over 50 events until I started running my signature one. From self-help/personal development, weight loss events, product development to finally writing a book in 48 hours. The more I spoke, the more confident I got, every event I could add more, not use notes, speak without too many nerves coming up and presented my offers with greater conviction and evidence. Don't give up too early. Learn, implement, review, repeat are the steps you need to embrace when it comes to event and retreats mastery. Use other people's stages to practise in the early days as they will get the bums on seats and then do some on your own. You will never regret becoming a great communicator and speaker. It is a skill that many fear, yet it provides opportunities you will never get one on one. It also makes you a more effective leader as a CEO and business owner because your team will benefit from your amazing communication skills and clarity of expression.

PART 2

LEVERAGE TO PROFIT

Now that we know what needs to happen to start monetising your book, it is time to become clever with your money and make every dollar you earn start producing profit. The key here is to look at your money beliefs, how you price yourself and learn ways to run a lean business. It doesn't matter if your total sales are huge, because in business it is the bottom line that matters the most. That bottom line is the thing that will get you to freedom.

Part 2 will delve into how to get organised, stay disciplined and the aspects you must track to become and remain highly profitable. Running a business is not an easy feat and you want to make sure your efforts reward you for the rest of your life. I feel one year running a business is like five years being an employee in someone else's company in terms of the effort, risk, discipline and focus that it takes. But also, one year in business can mean 10–20+ years of an annual income as an employee. The last eight years I have earnt in one year what I would have earnt in 20 years as a full-time employee in the optical industry. Something to think about … this can be you with the right tools, mindset and action in the next few years.

PART 2: LEVERAGE TO PROFIT

CHAPTER 18

PROFIT COMES FROM DISCIPLINE

Are you a great steward of your money? What is your money personality? What are your beliefs about money and how do you view those with wealth? Do you budget and know what your net worth is? There is so much involved in money and its management, as evidenced by the millions of books out there detailing these subjects. I know this because they happen to be among my favourite books to read.

I know I don't know everything about money, but through reading, employing financial experts as part of my team and being disciplined, I achieved financial independence by the age of 45. I started the journey at 33, so I may be a little older than those twenty-somethings who are already financially free, but you know what? I am super proud of myself. I did it in 12 years, starting with no network, no business experience, no business loan – just the thing between my ears, consistency, and a ton of discipline to get to where we are today. Oh, and I started the business with an 18-month-old baby, Judd, and then gave birth to my girls, Mika and Xara, during the hardest years, which were the first four years in the business. From year five, things became much easier, and we started living the lifestyle of our dreams and investing towards our financial independence goal.

Let's delve into how profit can become a reality in your life. Here are my top five strategies that I implement consistently. Discipline comes from consistency. You do it, even if you don't feel like it.

1. Get into the habit of monitoring your income and expenses weekly. At the start, there was an Excel spreadsheet template I would use. Nothing fancy, just

income, expenses and balance. That's it. There wasn't much to report on in the early days, but I would fill it out every Sunday, print it, and put it in a display folder so I could flick through the months and review. I didn't even have a proper accounting system when I started, just spreadsheets. You don't need anything fancy to be disciplined.
2. Draw up a budget – yet another spreadsheet. What is your current income, and what are your regular outgoings? Is there anything left over at the end? If there isn't, what can you cancel and do without to find some funds to invest in your business? And if there is a surplus, what can you invest in that will help you grow your money or your business? Do a budget at least once a year, or if you are growing rapidly, every three to six months, as things change. Once you have the first one done, reuse the template and just edit things in and out. Easy peasy.
3. Check your bank balances daily or a few times per week. This helps you visualise your money growing or helps you catch fraud very quickly. Trust me – it has happened to us more than eight times, and we have resolved it promptly. Also, this makes it very clear if you need to focus more on increasing cash flow. It's not fun looking at a low bank balance, but what you focus on expands.
4. Always pay off your credit card weekly. If you can, try not to owe anything to credit card companies. Buy things on credit so you can get your frequent flyer points that lead to free holidays, but at the end of each week, pay what you owe to your credit card. You don't want to be paying their crazy interest rates and eating away at your profits.
5. Keep your big money in an offset account. As you run your business and are on a path to making millions, your

big account will grow, and the best place to store this money as it comes in is an offset account. Our primary home is fully paid off, and the offset account now fully offsets our home on the Gold Coast in Australia. We don't rent out that home when we are not there, but it also doesn't cost us anything more to hold with a mortgage on it, as the mortgage is fully offset. Yes, I know I could put it on Airbnb and earn upwards of 40K passive annual income from it when we are not there, but for now, my husband and I are a bit precious about it. We set it up how we like it and don't want anyone there disturbing our vibe and causing wear and tear. That may change, but for now, it also acts as our Gold Coast headquarters and gives us a place to take our team for conferences and somewhere to stay when we do business in that state.

Profit is available to you. You just need to want to become a great manager of your money. You work hard for it, so why shouldn't it work hard for you? We only have so many productive years in our lives, and we want to be able to enjoy everything while we can, not when we are 80 and on the way out.

CHAPTER 19

DISCIPLINE COMES FROM BEING ORGANISED

My guess is that you brush your teeth every day. Perhaps you have great discipline and you do it twice – once in the morning and once at night. You learnt this skill when you were little and it stays with you for life. We often forget that just like to have healthy teeth we must brush daily, and so to have healthy profits you must action daily, weekly, monthly, quarterly, bi-annually and annual activities.

Remember – the money is in the SYSTEM. The activities are the process that makes the system stand and provide continuous profits. The majority of people approach life ad hoc and wonder why they have ad hoc results. They do something for a little while, get some results then stop, or worse, change to a new direction. Think of shopping at the supermarket. You buy your groceries and go to the checkout. All of a sudden you remember that you forgot an item. You step out of line and go to get it. You then return to the checkout and need to line up at the back of the line again. You then remember you forgot something else and the cycle repeats once again – all because you went shopping with no system and no list.

This is how the majority of people operate in life and keep wondering why they are not getting to the register – PROFIT! So, how do you get organised? I was actually planning to write a full book on this topic prior to this one as so many tell me how much they admire my organisational skills but I opted to do this one instead as it was more aligned with the focus and brand. Basically I have got into the line of teaching others how to write, publish and leverage their books and I am staying in that line. I am utilising the power of FOCUS and getting to my checkout time and time again.

Here are my top five organisational strategies:

1. I still use a physical diary that I write stuff into. I set my 90-day and 12-month goals at the back alongside my five-year vision and in my week per view I put my weekly goals and appointments. I do use an electronic diary as well, but I write everything into my physical one too. I designed and created this in 2016 and turned it into an evergreen version five years later. If you want one go to www.writeabook.com.au and look up the Ultimate Business Planner on my shop page. You can start using it at any time as it is evergreen and lasts for 15 months.

You just have to populate it with the current year – I show you how to do it and within 30–45 minutes you will be set for the next 15 months. I like to start a new one around November so that I have transitioned into the new year a bit earlier as it is easier for planning.

2. I use Mondays as a planning day for the week. It feels like the busiest day, but once I get everything set up, it is pure execution for the rest of the week. I do a weekly update, interview, coaching couch with Nat, team meeting, prep for workshops and events for the week and month all on a Monday. This way my team and my authors have what they need to get to work for the rest of the week.
3. I use a reminder app on my phone that keeps reminding me of important tasks, payments, follow-ups, etc. I know there are tons of apps that work as reminders so I won't recommend one here as it may be obsolete in the future. Find something that you can set up recurring reminders as well. The reason for this is that some things happen weekly, monthly, quarterly or annually. You don't want to have to reset this each time.
4. Declutter regularly. There are five key areas I recommend: your phone apps, your desktop, your email inbox and folders, your files on your computer and your physical space. You will find so much spare time when you free up your electronic and physical space. And the more room you open, the more room there is for your profits to soar. My family complete a 'mission declutter' at home once a year at the start of spring where we go through each and every drawer, cupboard and corner in the house and garage. Everyone has their dedicated area and we spend three days completing it. We order a skip so that we don't hold onto things because we don't have room in our bins. We donate, gift or throw out what we no longer need, want or use. The first time you do

this, you may take way longer than three days – it may in fact take three weeks of doing something every day, but trust me, it becomes so much easier when done each year. We also do mini declutters in between in areas we frequently use, like toiletries, the everything drawer, pantry or clothes. The kids were trained from babies and now they do their rooms independently. We even invented a mantra for it.

Mission Declutter Mantra:

The time has come to declutter
Each time I do it – it makes my heart flutter

No-one can scream
And there is no being mean

I let go of stuff I don't need
When I do this I feel freed

I donate to those with less
This makes my home free of mess

I make fast decisions
Which fulfil my visions

I take care of my space
And keep everything in its place

If there are no tantrums and stamping feet
When we finish it will be time for a tasty treat

5. Just like for your business systems, have life systems. We have travel packing systems, categorised folders for property, travel, utilities bills, business invoices, kids' school stuff, frequent flyer numbers for the full family. Everything in the home lives in categories that you can easily find and it makes sense where it is stored. Every mission declutter we fine-tune those systems or add to them to overcome frustrations we may have noticed lately.

We all have the same 24 hours in a day, but some people get a lot more shit done because they have multiple 'brushing teeth daily' strategies they deploy in their lives and businesses. If they are not great at something, they delegate and outsource it to someone that is, and they focus on their genius zone that ultimately will produce the greatest profits.

CHAPTER 20

LOVE MONEY

One of my mentors from my early years in business shared a very cool metaphor. He said think about your relationship with your partner. If you love them, you spend time with them, look after each other, support each other and plan the future together. In fact this is the same for any type of a relationship, parent and child, friendship or even boss and colleagues. In any of these if you don't show love and care for the people, in turn they will not show love and care back to you.

Which brings me to money. We all (like it or not) have a relationship with money. Some have a very volatile relationship, some love and hate, and others see it as dirty or slimy. My guess is, your viewpoint towards money will be reflected back into your life and bank balance. It's time to start loving money and building a wonderful marriage to it that will thrive until death do you part. This way money is going to start loving you back and profits will be plentiful as you start living the life of a rich author.

But, I hear you ask, how? You may have been raised a certain way and your parents told you certain things about money that are not serving you today. I know – that is most of us. Back in Macedonia there was a saying literally translated 'Money is a killer'. Geez talk about some disempowering language. Even a book was written with that title as it was such a common thing people said.

Thankfully, we are way more advanced now and have so many strategies available to us to rewire our thinking around money. One of my mentors is Denise Duffield-Thomas and she has two wonderful programs called Money Bootcamp and Sacred Money Archetypes I am a part of for life. If anyone can help you with this – it is her. She has been doing this work for over 20 years at the time of writing this book and always shares wonderful easy to understand content on the subject. Here are a handful of strategies I have learnt from her and other mentors over the years that have helped me bust my money limiting beliefs. Trust me, I am definitely not all healed when it comes to money, but I have come a long way from thinking it was a killer.

- Declutter regularly – there is an energy that is released when you do it that seems to attract new money. Denise also says 'shave your legs'. Funny, but often proven in her community.
- Reprogram your subconscious mind through regular affirmations and YouTube videos in the form of meditations. I laminated mine and put them in my shower in the early days and read them while brushing my teeth. With

meditations, I listen to one for 10 minutes on Monday to Thursday as I slowly wake for the day ahead.
- Read books about money.
- Set regular goals involving money and making sure you calibrate yourself towards achieving them. Sometimes we can go over the top and then be disappointed when it doesn't happen. Scale it back and also have the systems that will produce the money your goals are set around.
- Surround yourself with those that make more than you – remember you are the average of the five people around you. Start networking at places where you are not the smartest or richest person in the room.

This is plenty to get you started. Start with one and work your way down the list. Remember this needs to be a system in your life and you need to work at it on a regular basis. Massive results are only seen with consistency.

CHAPTER 21

GREATER RESPONSIBILITY = GREATER REWARDS

Don't wait! Don't wait to get picked, to get asked, to get invited, to get your business started, to get the promotion, to find the magic bullet. You are the magic bullet! No-one else is going to do the work you are meant to do. It's not easy. Anything worthwhile is a result of a journey or struggle, trials and tribulations. I don't know about you, but I want an extraordinary life, not just an average life. I want to experience as much as possible while I have the privilege to be on this earth. And I bet you are no different from me. After all you have picked up a book on this topic because you want more for yourself. It isn't enough to just tick off the bucket list that you have written a book. You want to help more people and in turn help yourself and your family live the life of your dreams.

This can be achieved by being a leader. Be the first one to say yes to opportunities and take the road least travelled. Responsibility is attached to leadership and so is success and rewards. Just think about the richest people that you know. They are not just responsible for themselves and their families. They are responsible for employees and properties, they lead organisations or countries, provide jobs and housing, invent systems that solve problems for the masses or entertain millions.

MJ Demarco says, 'If you want to make millions, help millions.' The more people you help achieve their dream, in turn your dreams will be taken care of. It's as easy as that. Well not quite, but it can be, through the power of your system and taking responsibility along the way. Rewards always flow fastest to those that have the courage to take a risk and take responsibility. It's kind of the universe rewarding the brave.

Start small and acclimatise every step of the way. You don't hire 10 employees at once when you start out. You get your first one and get used to that. Then you may be ready for the next and so on. Some people may move through the stages of growth a lot more rapidly, but no-one goes from no responsibility to an enormous amount of it. It should happen in stages so that as you grow you expand your circle of responsibility too. In fact, your systems must become way more sophisticated if you are to take on more responsibility and in turn manifest that into profits and rewards.

What does taking responsibility look like for the rich author:

- Saying 'yes' to speaking gigs and seeking them out at the start

- Going to networking events and following up first with those you meet
- Being consistent on social media and adding value to others with fresh content
- Building your online course and figuring it all out
- Reading books and learning from mentors – not expecting them to make you successful, but you are taking action from what they teach you
- Employing help where needed and paying your bills on time
- Hiring that venue, setting a day and running an event you organised from scratch
- Making an offer unashamedly
- Innovating and thinking on new solutions to your challenges
- Not being scared to ask for help when you are stuck.

The more responsibility you take, the greater the rewards you will experience. Sometimes responsibility can be closely connected to risk-taking. However, the better educated you are, the lower the likelihood is of you taking risks that don't work out in your favour. Make education your lifelong university. Informed decisions are always more likely to have a positive outcome over ones you have just taken a punt on. Will you be safe from risk if you educate yourself regularly? No, you will still make mistakes and fail, however they may not be as detrimental as the ones you may have taken uninformed.

CHAPTER 22

KNOW YOUR NUMBERS

How much does it cost to run your business? What does it cost to find a client? What do you need to hit every week to just break even?

What does it cost to run your life and the lives of your families? If you have employees, how much do you pay out in wages?

These are all really important numbers to familiarise yourself with. That's why in an earlier chapter I recommended starting to track your income and expenses and draw up your budget regularly. This is what will help you understand in every $1 you earn how much you get to keep as profit.

My accountant has a pie chart he shows us at the end of our tax planning or tax time meetings which highlights how much of the pie goes to wages, advertising, travel and other bits. The best and biggest bit however has always been our profit slice. I love seeing this pie chart towards the end of our meetings. It confirms to me that I am running a lean business (we will talk about that more in the next chapter) and that we have the funds to invest in our future.

For now, I really just want you to avoid playing the game 'ignorance is bliss'. This is why so many businesses fail in the first 12 months and most in the first three years. They pull the wool over their eyes and live in 'hope world' that everything will work out. When it doesn't, they make a decision that they just weren't cut out to be a business owner. What a BS story that is! Feeding yourself impossibilities is really demeaning and sad. You can do this. You just didn't know how – if you knew you would have done better. As you are reading this book, you know better so I suggest do better.

Where to start knowing your numbers I hear you ask? Open your internet banking and start there, look over your past six months of transactions and categorise them into different types of spending: groceries, utilities, travel, petrol, fun, clothing, business bills, etc. This will not only help you with your budget, it will also be a great reality check on how and on what you spend your money.

You may discover unused subscriptions you are still paying for and money leaks you didn't know existed. Just yesterday here it was the end of financial year, and on July 1 the new financial year began. I actually love doing my bookkeeping alongside my mum who helps us. Every first of the month we need to import the Visa statement and reconcile the personal and business expenses. As we spend everything on the Visa to earn Qantas Frequent Flyer points there is a lot to go through each month. As I do it monthly, I can still remember what happened and what each transaction was for. In this one month, I found two subscriptions that I didn't know about. I addressed it with the family and we cancelled them out immediately. That was $35 that should not have been spent, but I caught it early and it stayed that way not turning into $420 if I didn't notice it for 12 months.

This is also connected closely to taking responsibility. Knowing your numbers means you are acting as a grown up and managing your money with smarts. The universe doesn't give more money to bad money managers as it recognises that if it gives you more and you don't know how to manage it, you will get into trouble with it. Makes sense right?

Second thing to do is develop the weekly habit of tracking what comes in and out and to look at your bank accounts daily. As your business grows you will need to track more things so again, you will acclimatise yourself with less tracking and build on it as you grow.

Numbers are fun and you know what they say – money makes money so when your numbers grow you can have a lot more fun compounding the amount of money that you earn and that you get to keep.

CHAPTER 23

RUN A LEAN BUSINESS

The secret to a very profitable business is your ability to run a lean operation and still provide the support and value to your clients. It's not about cutting corners and doing a half assed job but knowing where 80% of your results come from and eliminating 20% of the fluff that sucks money out of your business but doesn't bring in revenue.

I call this 20% the 'money suckers' that you may not be ready yet to spend money on, but you do anyway in the hope you will look or grow bigger faster. Here are some money suckers I want you to avoid if you are in the first five years of business:

- Fancy branding at a level that corporations get for your one-man/woman show
- Overinvesting in mentors and programs in a constant search of the magic bullet that will make you rich quick. There is no such thing, so stop looking. Use what you have invested in and limit yourself to one mentor and one program per year. Do not stop investing ever in education or mentorship, just don't do it all at once as it is tempting to say yes to everything when you are not making as much money and you are desperate
- Hiring someone too soon or locally. Your first hire should be a VA (Virtual Assistant). There are plenty offshore for a quarter of the price. Go and read my book *Me and my VA* that I co-wrote with my virtual assistant Lendy. She has been with me for nearly nine years and was my first employee I ever hired. It is written from both perspectives – the VA and the business owner. I must admit I hired her two years too late but I did have my

husband come in before her so in a way he was a free VA to me for a while. LOL.
- Buying every paid subscription that will help your business and having a ton of recurring monthly expenses. There are so many free versions of every tool that you do not always need the paid one. We still use the free versions of Slack (team communication), Asana (project management), basic Dropbox (only $170/year) and, up until recently, free Canva (DIY graphic design). Look out for systems that are being developed now that have multiple solutions in one place rather than needing to buy them separately. Tekmatix is an all-in-one business and course platform that includes a CRM, AI assistant bot, calendars, courses and memberships hosting, websites, funnels, forms, quizzes, affiliate manager, email marketing, automation, project management, task management, contracts, invoicing, quoting, social media scheduler and much more ... with 24-hour support. Check it out via this link https://bit.ly/tekmatixnat
- Buying done-for-you marketing and sales early on. These two departments should always be the final two that are outsourced in a business. If you don't know how to market and sell for your business, how the hell are you going to instruct others to do it on your behalf? I know, everyone wants to avoid these two, but they are unavoidable if you want to run a lean business for a long time. These services are not guaranteed and they will only be as good for you as you are. Tens of thousands of dollars have been blown like this by inexperienced new authors or business owners.

If you are going to invest in something to grow your business, always do your due diligence. Don't rely on the company to sell themselves to you. Go to their clients and ask how it was working with them.

Don't just ask the company to speak to one of their clients, but choose from their website someone at random. I always tell my aspiring authors to do due diligence even on us. Go to my website, look at the bookshelf of authors and contact whoever you like. I know with confidence we have helped so many people that love us and will speak highly of us. I don't need to choose who people can speak to. My clue that we are doing a great job is also the fact we have our clients return to publish book two and three – and this year seems to have turned into the year of book four. It's so cool to have a community that is so loyal and happy. It makes my heart sing when I know my team has done an excellent job and our clients choose us over and over again. This is what continues to make our business lean. Repeat business doesn't cost a cent and is so much less time consuming. Our back-end sales are 35% of our annual revenue – how cool is that?

CHAPTER 24

HIGHER REVENUE DOESN'T MEAN HIGHER PROFITS

Yes, you read that right! You can have a 10M business and only profit 500K or you can have a 2M business and profit 1M. What? How can that be? Well, it goes back to how lean you are running your business. Are you throwing all your revenue around just to look big or are you being smart, keeping it smaller and enjoying higher profits with less responsibility? Remember more money will mean more responsibility.

We will talk in a later chapter about what is enough for you. This is always so different for different people. Everyone has a number where they decide that is enough for their dream life. For some it is 100K and for some 100M or 1B. It all depends on your goals and dreams. What I am always looking to achieve in my business is quality over quantity. I prefer to invest time in training and development of my team so that I only need one or two team members per department that are well engaged and rockstars in their roles. I look to create lots of bonding opportunities where we plan, play and produce amazing memories and strategies for the business in the months and years ahead.

Each year we have grown by one team member consistently as we have set up more systems and as a pathway to having my business being able to run successfully without me in the near future. I am proud to say that in the 14 years not one team member has left our business. We had a few false starts with sales reps while we were learning what would work for us in starting to grow the sales department, otherwise everyone else has been around for years. From the first team member nine years ago, all the others who have joined the team have stayed on. This means we have an experienced team that displays consistency and stability for our clients. The interesting thing is that a huge percentage of our clients remain in our community for many years and write multiple books as a result.

The secret to higher profits is relationships. Amazing relationships with your team members and clients is key. That way the business does not continuously have to churn through HR resources or spend huge amounts on marketing to keep finding new clients. Each dollar takes you a lot further and you can invest on refining other areas to make it even nicer for your people.

I believe profitability is a lot more important than net sales. It is only with high profits that you can invest and build out your millionaire lifestyle. It is truly empowering knowing your 'enough' numbers. Another way we look at it is – how many brand-new authors do we need to be helping each year to maintain our level of business? That number for us is 100. We also track this, as we know if we get to know

100 new authors each year, we maintain our business at a consistent level that we want. Trust me, maintenance is not an easy feat. Just because you get to a certain level of success doesn't mean it will be easy to stay there. Customers, the marketplace, technology and how people make buying decisions is consistently changing and innovation and pivoting must be a necessary practice in your business. How we spoke to our aspiring authors 10 years ago, to how we delivered five years ago and today is hugely varied by what the world was going through and how fast technology was changing our way of being to reach our ideal clients.

Don't ever stop learning and investing in yourself. As you help yourself, you will be able to help others and when you help others, you get to enjoy the benefits of that. Money doesn't come to those that do not add value to the world and help solve problems.

If your business is not profitable, are you too cheap? Are you unaware of what your breakeven point is for your business to succeed and stay open? It is super important to calibrate your numbers correctly and to be consistently increasing your prices. Everything in the world goes up over time. Why should you not do the same for your products and services?

Always remember – higher revenue does not mean higher profits!!!

CHAPTER 25

AUTOMATE AS MUCH AS POSSIBLE

I touched on in the previous chapter that I am working on replacing myself out of my business so that it can run without being business owner reliant. After all, that is when you truly can call yourself a business owner. If you must work in your business to generate revenue or deliver aspects of it, you still are considered partly self-employed. Don't get me wrong, I love my business and doing some work within it, however I also know that I want to build it for exit one day.

As I am writing this chapter from Bali, I have just completed two weeks of school holidays with my kids enjoying time together without any interruptions or business distractions. My team also generated over 50K in sales without me. We do this three or four times a year and collectively I have around four months off during a 12-month period. So how does this happen when the business still needs me for some things? It boils down to three strategies for me:

1. Automation using online tools
2. Human resources
3. Systems creation.

So many of us, get stuck in the mindset of 'I can do it best and fastest so I may as well just do it', that we become slaves to our business. This can only lead to exhaustion and poor customer service when you become super busy. You cannot do every role in your business the best. I bet you don't even love doing some of the tasks, but you do them because you feel you must.

For me admin was the first thing I needed off my plate so that I can focus more on revenue and sales to grow further and faster. Then came the publishing company and I needed a team member to deal with the detail and project management of that department. As it grew fast, we ended up getting a second person in that department within 12 months. These two amazing ladies do a much better job than I can and bounce off each other for support. When one is away, the other one holds the fort. I certainly was not a big fan of the detailed work. These team members are also responsible for customer service. My husband took author prep sessions off me and took our marketing department in-house after training under people we paid for marketing. That now saves us over 60K each year.

Finally, it was time to look at building out a sales team so I can be removed from the final key role in the business. As I said we had three false starts until we learnt the type of people that would be best for this role and for our business. This department is now established with two great sales book strategists, and the full team has been working diligently on systemising their roles with the guidance of our systems champion project managing us all.

Remember what I have been saying the whole way through this book – the money is in the systems. By documenting how we do everything in every role and department, the systems can then be duplicated and learned easily if there is staff turnover, or we decide to sell and exit.

Nowadays I am responsible for being the face of the business, doing some training delivery for our authors which is my favourite and really being the innovator and problem solver. Your aim is to become the brains and mastermind to your enterprise. Your thinking is where you will make the most money. Your relationships are where you will engage and keep everyone around you. Start today! Automate what you can, hire slow and train thoroughly, and then write out your systems for your ultimate freedom to become a reality.

My recommendation is that you outsource lower-level activities like admin, bookkeeping and customer service first and then marketing followed by sales being the last one that ever gets replaced. Even nowadays I still am involved in some of the sales, as aspiring authors are buying me and my system and some even request to chat to me. I am okay with this as I know this role is something I enjoy and am great at. The best thing though is when I take my mini-retirements during those four months each year, I do not need to do anything for the business as it can keep running without me.

PART 2: LEVERAGE TO PROFIT

CHAPTER 26

FASTRACK WITH AI – LESS HUMAN RESOURCES

So much can be written about AI and people are certainly bringing out books by the truckloads on this topic that you can explore in much greater detail, but here I just want to share some of the amazing benefits that have saved me and my team tons of time. First, I want to share the fact that AI should not be used to write your book or even your content. The reason for this is that it cannot ever communicate the way you do or express personal stories that you only know. Yes, AI can be trained and it is improving as each day goes by, however I don't believe it can ever feel authentically you.

In saying that here are some key areas we have been able to save so much time when we have used the help of AI in our business:

- Writing awkward emails – this is my number one game changer of late. What used to take sometimes one or two hours to compose, read and re-read happens in only 10 minutes max with some instructions given to ChatGPT and its professional output. I put in my flavour and press send
- Brainstorming content ideas on my expertise when I get stuck on ideas about what videos to film and what content to write about. I take the idea I like most and run with my own flavour on it
- Basic copyediting of my written content without changing any of my style or structure
- Marketing titles, ideas and copywriting starting points that I then write in my own words
- Using it as the search engine Google – I actually go to ChatGPT more now than I go to Google for answers

- Using the 'speak to' app on my phone and having a conversation with it as I may need to problem-solve or brainstorm something
- Creating illustrations with written instructions inside the Canva AI
- Writing out business systems a lot faster.

The key is to have it open all day as you are working away at your stuff. Get into the habit of going to it for answers and advice. You will increase you and your team's productivity in no time. You want to train everyone to have the same strategy with it and demonstrate uses that you discover helpful.

Next level to all of this is creating your own GPT Assistant. This is part of ChatGPT where you program a GPT Assistant with information about what you need it to be. I have one that is an 'email subject line wizard', another one that I use to copyedit in my flavour and another one that is a 'marketing machine' that can spit out a blog, email and social media content on a topic I give it.

The point of a GPT Assistant is to not have to prompt it all the time from scratch. It basically is programmed to know your business, clients and detailed information about what you do and how you do it. Some companies out there help businesses with very sophisticated GPT Assistants that become a replacement for real people in specific roles. They can be customer service, sales or marketing focused. If you think about how apps became something people created for their businesses, so are GPT Assistants – they are the new app. You can do basic ones for free with ChatGPT yourself or for more in depth and sophisticated ones you want to work with a provider that can help you develop it top notch.

The one-off investment in this could mean replacing two or three human resource positions within your company. This is all going to become bigger and better as the months roll on. AI is growing and learning at an unprecedented speed, so do not get left behind by ignoring what is already here. Your competitors will overtake you in an instant if you don't implore the power of AI.

CHAPTER 27

BUILD A BUFFER – PLAN FOR DOWNTURNS

I trust by now you know how important profits are to sustain your business and build your millionaire lifestyle. In Part 3 we will be talking about where to spend and invest your profits, but before that, it's important we talk about building your buffer so that you never feel caught off guard. It's never too early or too late to start.

Most people have at best three months of savings to survive on their current lifestyle. When I think of this, I feel scared for them. When the global pandemic hit in 2020 it took more than two years for things to come back to some kind of normal. I know even in the third year there were massive shifts in the economy with interest rates skyrocketing and causing changes in people's buying behaviour.

This is one thing that was instilled in me from a little kid that was positive about money – saving for a rainy day. Or as my mum says, 'having a black fund'. By being a business owner your buffer must end up being substantial so that in times where there are downturns you can survive the hit and keep your people and clients.

Downturns, pandemics, global financial crisis, price hikes, interest rate rises will undoubtably happen. We often won't know when but they are a guarantee – just like death and taxes. So, how do you start to build your buffer? Well you don't spend all that you earn. Keep some of your profits and continue making your big account bigger. I remember mine was only a few thousand dollars when I began and when it hit 100K it was a massive achievement. From there I just kept going. The most it ever got to is 1.4M!

Now you are probably thinking – why am I keeping so much cash in the bank? Even some of my financial experts have said I don't need that much. Well, the way I look at it is that I run a business and cash is king. I want to be able to tap into large sums of money if I need it fast. I also use that money to offset a full property we own on the Gold Coast in Australia. We purchased this at the start of the pandemic before prices skyrocketed on the Gold Coast and now have had it basically for free for more than four years. It's 820K mortgage is fully offset and now it's worth more than 1.3M three years later.

My big account is now down to 850K because I used some of the cash to buy another property. It paid for 50% of it and it will be a huge cashflow positive outcome when its built due to the strategy behind it. In the mortgage set up of this, there was a delay and for some reason we had to come up with 500K to pay for the land in 24 hours otherwise we were going to be fined big time. Guess what – we walked into the bank and had it sorted in 20 minutes and avoided this hefty fine.

Building a buffer for unexpected situations, economic downturns and general slower business times is how you survive and stay around for the long haul. Look at your breakeven point, know your lifestyle budget and live and spend below your means. Your buffer will save your butt and make you feel so much at peace when shit hits the fan. You are in business, and you need access to cash. Be smart with your money and know that you work really hard for it, so allow it to work hard in return for you.

PART 2: LEVERAGE TO PROFIT

CHAPTER 28

BUILD A FAMILY (YOUR TEAM AND CLIENTS)

I touched on this in an earlier chapter, but I want to unpack this deeper here for you. Most likely my guess is that you will end up spending as much time talking to your team and clients as you do your family over the time that you work together. In some situations and times, even more than your family. So why would you not build in activities and experiences similar to what you would do with your family?

The benefit of this is that when people feel like family, they start treating you and the business as if it is their own. This in itself is huge. It's hard to find great staff and even harder for them to care as much as you do. But taking an interest in their lives, creating experiences and having things to relate on outside of business operations is huge. Similar things apply when you think of your clients. Some of my clients have become super close family friends, other business owners that I collaborate with and people I catch up with when I am in their city on my travels.

Here are some ideas of how I have been able to develop quality over quantity when it comes to team and client relationships:

- Every Monday at our team meeting we share the best thing that happened on the weekend so we know more about each other outside of work
- Every two or three months we do an activity together for the day. At times, we have even gone away on a weekend together
- Once a year we spend 10 days at my Gold Coast house bonding and conferencing around the business
- We plan lunches and dinners for authors whenever we are in their city

- I have put on group book launches to celebrate authors
- Even when we travel internationally we always make the effort to see people even just for a couple of hours – sometimes we only meet our clients online and never know them in real life so this takes the relationship to the next level
- The past two years I've also developed a Bond & Beyond International retreat for seven days charging only cost price for the stay so that we can all connect somewhere central in the world and authors meet one another in real life and simply bond and connect
- During the pandemic I started FriYaY night drinks on Zoom and we caught up for the first 12 months weekly – we have kept up this tradition now four years on, but we now meet once a month on the first Friday of the month for a general catch up and chit chat with only a social purpose behind it
- We follow each other and support each other's posts on social media so we know what is going on in each of our lives.

You may think, well how does this bring more revenue into the business. All these activities have no real business transaction attached to it. You are right – they don't. What they do have is good will, relationship building and maintenance and show how much we care for our team and clients. There was a quote I heard a while back – 'People don't care how much you know, until you can show them how much you care.'

I've noticed now, years later, the outcome of all these activities. It may not be immediate but it's enormous in hindsight. Team members that don't leave my side, protect me and my business. Clients that are loyal and continue to buy from us to publish more than just one book. Some are at their third and fourth books and are entrenched into our community for six plus years and going strong. Collaborative relationships that have resulted in so many sales to brand new authors that we didn't yet have trust with. Opportunities, ideas and tips that a single person cannot come up with by themselves. I can keep going but I think you get my point. Treat people like family and soon enough they will treat you and your business the same.

CHAPTER 29

BUILD A GLOBAL BRAND (LOCAL, NATIONAL, THEN INTERNATIONAL)

New authors that I meet always say they want their message to have global impact. This a wonderful intention to set and certainly one that will give you the most leverage, however, to reach this status there is a process you must go through. People don't just go international overnight – certainly there are the small one in a million cases where something makes them go viral, but in the majority of cases this is not how it happens.

I always say that you need to become famous first offline then online. First in your local city, state, country and then international. Your impact expands the more your grow as a thought leader and entrepreneur. So, why does it happen much slower than people would like it to happen? It goes back to relationships once again. It takes time to establish rapport and trust with people that will give you opportunities or promote you.

You must prove yourself first that you are serious about your expansion and helping people. When you start you have no testimonials, no credibility and no-one knows you from a bar of soap. Those that write books with already established brands and reputations can fast-track the time it takes to reach global impact but that is because they began years ago and they are now leveraging relationships started years ago.

If you are anything like me and are starting from scratch, then you have a few years ahead of you to build a network that is ultimately going to impact your net worth. My strategy that I used in my first 12 months was based on advice I was given by my coaching school when I began 14 years ago. They told me to get out there in my local city and attend two networking events each week.

I was to meet people, look at ways I can help and continue showing up. This in turn helped me refine my niche, build my confidence around new people in strange new places who seemed so at ease and relaxed about networking. I felt too young, too inexperienced and like a fraud. However I committed to those two events every week and every time I would show up it would become easier, I would run into some of the same people and the more they saw me and I saw them the more trust and relationships we developed.

So when my first book came out, it wasn't just that I became an author and generated six figures over the next 12 months, but those relationships at the events I attended came to fruition. Those people were my initial supporters for my book, that asked me to speak at their health and wellness practices to their clients and introduced me to future potential collaborative partners.

Relationships and a book is how the magic happens! So if you have not yet written your book or are in the midst of it, start going to events, being seen and build rapport with people. Everything else afterwards will be much easier and monetisation of your efforts will happen a lot faster.

As time progresses, continue asking for testimonials, reviews and recommendations. Some of your best clients will be sending you new clients and word of mouth will become a huge way you will win over new business. However, never stop marketing to a new audience if you want to grow bigger with intention. The way we went national and international was through the power of Facebook ads and our million-dollar winning seminar formula. Those clients now send us new aspiring authors because we focus on our relationship with them long term.

PART 3

PROFIT TO FREEDOM

The final piece of the puzzle is here: buying your way to freedom and not having to work all the time. You have learnt how to be clever with your money and keep your profits, but cash by itself won't multiply your money as fast the strategies we will talk about in this next part can. Cash declines in value due to inflation and due to the fact countries keep printing more money each year.

It is time to start doing what the rich do and invest your profits into assets that will appreciate over time and grow your money tree bigger and bigger each year. I remember I set a goal at the age of 35, two years after I started my business that I would love to be financially independent by the time I am 45. At the time my net worth was less than 200K as we had a small amount of equity in our home. As the business grew, we invested year after year our profits into assets that appreciate over time. When I turned 45, we had our annual meeting with our financial advisor Claudia. I asked her this question: are we financially independent? At this time, we were still running our business full time and certainly there wasn't a ton of passive income from our properties, but the equity in all of them was massive and our primary home and another property were fully paid off. She basically said, if you were to sell everything today and invest that money into something that produces 8% returns a year (very realistic), you will get more than enough passive income to live the lifestyle you live without having to work another day. BOOM!!! I did it – I was so proud of myself that day.

This didn't stop me from continuing to run the business and I didn't retire soon after. It actually put a fire in my belly to set the next goal – $10M net worth. I have set a new milestone: building generational wealth. More on that in the chapters that follow. Let's get into it …

PART 3: PROFIT TO FREEDOM

CHAPTER 30

YOUR FINANCIAL INDEPENDENCE TEAM

Unless you studied accounting, real estate, financial planning or anything that has to do with knowing how to make your money work for you, you will need some help. Even if you did study in some of these areas, it's not possible to be proficient in all of them. These experts that can help you with your money are worth every dollar you will pay for their service. But you must select carefully and do your due diligence.

I remember when we started out, we had an accountant that was a golf buddy of my husband and we went to him the first few years in business until I realised that I was correcting him and picking up things he had missed. Also, he never spoke strategy and drove a beat-up Datsun. That should have been a sign that we weren't going to get ahead having him as our accountant. So we changed to someone that was already a partner in his firm, who I had gotten to know well through networking, and who I knew was already working with other very successful business owners. He worked in a very nice office, had property investments and drove a Ferrari.

We have been with him for nearly a decade now and together have grown in our strategies, how we protect the business and ourselves and have implemented many different ways to minimise our taxes in a legal way. Don't get me wrong, I actually love paying tax and always pay on time or early, as I know it means we are making money and also because I don't want to feel like I owe anyone anything. But there are ways that us normal people (not accountants) don't know how to manage our tax affairs. Find yourself a rockstar accountant and what you pay in larger fees for them, you will save in tax dollars because of their expert knowledge on taxes. After all, you are a business owner now and there are perks available to you that you should be taking advantage of.

Next is you mortgage broker and/or property broker. I've had mine close to 13 years now and similar to my accountant and financial advisor I found them all whilst networking. Those regular meetings I used to see them at developed such like, know and trust that working with them was a no-brainer. I always feel like I have friends helping me when it comes to financial decisions and strategies. You want a mortgage broker that has properties themselves. After all if you want to build a portfolio with great properties learn from someone that is ahead of you. I remember in the early years asking my mortgage broker how many properties he owned to which he replied 34 nonchalantly. He is such a great guy and so humble, I wanted to be just like him when I grew up.

He also introduced me to a buyer's advocate that helped me buy a couple of properties that I didn't have time to find myself. Same thing happened with a couple of other ones that my mortgage broker suggested. Since then I have also used a commercial buyer's advocate and mortgage broker that I fully trust.

My final person that is part of my financial independence team is my financial advisor Claudia. She is a little older than me and a powerhouse of a woman that also became financially independent in her early forties. She drives a Porsche and only works because she just loves being a financial advisor. I also want to be her when I grow up, so it was a no-brainer to hire her. Every year she meets with us, prepares statements of advice and also shares strategies for us to continue growing and saving on tax.

You are probably thinking — what about your bookkeeper Nat? Well I don't have one as I love doing that myself. I have trained my mum on some aspects and we do it together. I like numbers and keeping my pulse on them, but if you don't I suggest that you find a great one.

So where should you start? Here are my top tips:

- Ask for recommendations from those that you trust
- Meet and interview potential advisors you like the sound of and ask for reviews. If allowed, ask them if it's okay to speak to one of their clients
- Ask those that you are considering what their results are in that area you are looking to hire them. They may not reveal it, in which case I would not go with them and if they do and it's not where you are headed then I suggest finding someone different
- Go networking and simply start getting to know people by seeing them regularly. Build trust and go through all the above due diligence to choose smart
- Do not stay with someone out of loyalty, always look for results and growth. After all these are the people that help you with the growth of your money tree and the least amount of loss of leaves over time
- Look at what car they are driving. LOL.

CHAPTER 31

RETIRING FAMILY

Two of my proudest moments since I became a business owner are the day that I told my husband to quit his day job and come into the business with me and the day I told my mum to quit her day job and in a way retire while lending me a bit of support with small tasks around the business and with our children.

I remember 18 months before my husband quit his day job, another woman business owner announcing that her husband had just quit and they were now going to fend for themselves with their business. In that moment I thought and said quietly to myself: 'When will I be writing a social media post like this?' That little desire was born within me and I just kept doing my best to continue growing. There have been a few moments like this where that quiet internal voice wonders about how and when something significant will happen and you know what – it does!!! Sooner or later, desire turns into its physical manifestation.

It's been almost 12 years since Stuart quit his day job and seven years since my mum did and we truly are a family business and not just supporting our family but also the families of our employees and contractors. It is so rewarding knowing that this business has grown bigger than me and is now a support system for so many that earn from it and so many that use its products and services.

My husband and mum are not retired doing nothing at all, however they never have to answer to another boss – except for me. I am a very nice boss to them both and my team ☺. We all love contributing and helping in whatever way we can and do really feel close and enjoy achieving things together.

So how do you do this for yourself? Well the first step is to retire yourself from your day job. How I did that was to work out a figure that I needed to hit consistently for three months until I would hand in my resignation. That figure for me was twice my weekly income from my day job. Say I was earning $500 a week, I needed to generate $1000 on average a week over 12 weeks from my business consistently so that I know I can cover everything and more and also plan for any lower sales periods where that average may drop.

PART 3: PROFIT TO FREEDOM

For my husband it was very similar – we needed the business to be bringing in twice his income over three months from his day job and it happened to be a time when his employer gave him an ultimatum at Christmas 2012 – either move to another retail store as a manager or quit. This other store was an extra 45 minutes' drive, collectively a 90-minute drive each way to get to. We did our numbers and took the leap of faith. It was really scary the first year but we adjusted, he worked on his employee to business owner mindset and we have never looked back.

For my mum it was a bit different. We got super busy and I felt I needed Stuart to come and do the national event tours I was running as I was missing opportunities being on my own. People would walk out of my seminars as they could not talk to me at the end – I only had time to chat to two or three people. With Stuart we could do up to eight after a seminar. Our events grew bigger and it was a much better idea to have a buddy, support person and someone you can vent to on the road.

So we told Mum what we wanted to do and asked her if she would quit her full-time job and come and help us at ad hoc times with the kids and other small roles in the business and we would pay her the exact same wage she was earning in her day job. For her it was really scary how this would look like, but she trusted me and took the leap of faith to join our team. Seven years on, none of us have ever looked back. We do what we want, when we want and travel wherever we want. My mum comes to some of our family holidays as the kids truly see her as the third parent and she is super funny and entertaining to have around. Stu and I can go on date nights and often we take trips alone for pleasure while mum stays and lives in with the kids. This happens two or three times a year.

Retiring family is not easy, but so rewarding and why would you not? If you get along with your family, it's one of the best things you could do to help them and bring them in on the journey. You can all problem-solve, discuss growth and understand what it's like in the good times and the challenging times. Always discuss this before you make decisions and make sure everyone is comfortable with the change and move you are about to make. Not everyone is cut out for uncertainty and being their own boss – sometimes it works out amazing like for us and sometimes you need to make new decisions so that everyone is happy with what they are doing.

Doing it together is what brings the freedom piece together with less effort as everyone is on a similar schedule if under the same business model.

CHAPTER 32

SHOULD YOU RETIRE?

This is one question that I have pondered on for last five years. Why do people retire? What would I do if I retired? How much money would I need if I was to retire to do all that I want? And then Christmas and summer comes in Australia all at the same time and for about six weeks I have a little taste of what retirement would look like. I take pretty much the last three weeks in December and first three weeks in January off.

It's lovely as it is summer, we are all distracted by all the activities with the kids on school holidays, but even that gets tiring towards the end. I start to feel like I have been laying around, reading books, eating, drinking and simply overindulging for way too long. I feel sluggish and like I am not adding value to anyone. Maybe it's just me, but there is only so much sitting around one person can do. I am number one for taking regular holidays and breaks and they do add up to around four months each year, so I do love the breaks. But I don't think I can do it permanently.

I have also thought about this when it comes to observing other financially independent and successful people in the world. Ones I know and ones I don't know personally – celebrities or big-time entrepreneurs. I often think – they don't have to work anymore, so why do they? What keeps them going at the intensity they do? There must be more to this. What I have deducted from observations and personal experience is that we keep working to feel of value, to contribute and be of service to others. We feel happy when we help others – it's a deeply ingrained human need.

Why do you think so many retirees pass away not too long after retiring? Loss of purpose is a real thing. It is really sad, they lose their identity and worth by doing nothing. To me this is a scary concept. I never what to have nothing to do. I am an achiever at heart and love feeling productive. I love being told how helpful my business is to people and how much time and money it has saved or made them.

So, I have decided – I am never retiring. I may slow down or pivot in the way I contribute to this world and the people in it, but I will be teaching for as long as I know and mentoring the future generations so they evolve to the next level faster than me. What about you? I'd love to know your thoughts on retirement as it is one subject that always makes me curious – email me at natasa@natasadenman.com and let me know your views on it. Put in the subject line 'Retirement' so I can pick it up amongst all the other emails that come in.

CHAPTER 33

WHAT IS ENOUGH?

I said earlier in the book that we will be discussing this, and that time has arrived. What is your 'enough' number? Do you know what you need to live off and still have all the time, experiences, things and people you love at your disposal? This number is different for everyone. For some it will be 100K a year passive income, for others 500K, while for others it's in the millions or more. We know there are approximately 3000 billionaires in the world so they have a huge 'enough' number in comparison to more regular people.

It doesn't make you more or less important depending on what that number is. The most important thing is to know yours. What is the number where you will feel at peace knowing everything is taken care off and you can do as you please. There is a simple financial independence formula whereby you work out your annual expenses and then multiply them by 25 or 30 to account for a safety margin.

Annual expenses are things like housing, food, entertainment, travel, transportation, insurance, etc. If you did the budget I suggested in earlier chapters then you should be able to work it out easily. For me I worked on 200K per year x 25 = $5M for financial independence status. This may change but that was my dream figure for the past five years that I hit.

Yours may be lower or higher. Another decision my husband and I have made a while back was the fact that we have no desire to grow our business any bigger than it currently is. We are at a multi seven-figure level and we have an intimate community of amazing authors that we service at a world class level and they keep us busy writing and publishing multiple books. We love depth and longevity with our authors and our team if you have not picked that up by now.

The intimacy of it all keeps things simple and gives us flexibility in our lifestyle to make quick decisions and live by design and choice and not something that feels like we must do.

Aside from your 'enough' number, think about what is 'enough' when it comes to your total revenue, profit, team, holidays you take each year, physical exercise you do, car that you drive, etc. For example, seven years ago I decided to put exercise in my top three values as I want to live longer, stay as energetic as I am and have mental clarity and capacity to do as much as I can. My 'enough' number for that is that I exercise four times each week Monday to Thursday. I have kept this up 95% of the time alongside two personal trainers that have worked with me over the years (twice a week with my PT and twice a week on my own often completing an intense seven-minute workout which is an app on my phone). If I am not well I have a break, if I am away I often exercise more on holidays as a gym is generally nearby and I find it gives me a great sense of achievement as I embark on a day of fun and relaxation.

Think about all sorts of areas of your life. Drinking is another thing. I don't want to fully stop having a drink so I say once or twice a week is enough. Yes on holidays we do it more often and when on a detox I may have a month off. It's not a about being perfect, it's about knowing what's enough and sometimes colouring outside the lines of that for special circumstances.

Knowing your 'enough' number is very empowering and when you hit them and stay consistent you feel in control and like you can do anything. Your 'enough' numbers may change as you grow older and change your values so feel free to reassess and set new ones. It is when you don't know that you are most in danger of floundering and not reaching your destination.

CHAPTER 34

BUY BACK YOUR TIME

One thing that will eat away a significant portion of your profits will be when you start hiring staff for your business. It is a very big and scary step when you onboard your first employee and you know their livelihood lies in your hands moving forward. This is also your first step to removing yourself and creating a true business that is not business owner reliant. Celebrate this moment as you are now starting to buy back your time.

My best advice on this is to start slow and go steady. Get used to paying another wage before you put another person on. I've seen too many cases where people have hired too many employees too fast and crashed and burned having to let them all go. Outsourcing and delegating is great but also having the systems and revenue to support this is key. You want your team to stick for the long haul so take your time with each of them as you train them to do things exactly how you created them.

By going slower, you are able to also provide better service to your existing clients and retain them long term as well. As much as we all want to be as profitable as possible, at some point you will start to value your time way more than money. Time with your loved ones, time for things that you love to do for leisure and time to just be and do whatever you set your mind to.

Start to separate your business from needing you all the time. This is the order I would recommend that you start outsourcing: first to go is admin to a virtual assistant or personal assistant, next bookkeeping (unless you love doing it like me), after that customer service and some delivery that others can do on your behalf, then comes marketing and finally sales.

One big mistake I see a lot of business owners do is outsource marketing and sales too early and burn a lot of cash (as these two are more expensive to outsource) without any significant results. Big MISTAKE!!! After all, you are the thought leader, and in the early days people will be buying you and you know best how to market your product or service. So while you outsource all the rest, you make more time and space for more marketing and sales.

We are super blessed that my husband was trained by our Facebook ads team we outsourced to for six years and the past five years he has been doing it in-house for us. Myself, I have been in a marketing/face of the business and sales role the whole time I've had the business. It is only in the past two-and-a-half years we put on our first salesperson and recently added a second one as now I am required more for the ideas, innovations, problem-solving and training and development of my team. My time is spent more in meetings and training over sales calls. That's what my team is for. So now when I go on holidays, I no longer need to do any business tasks as we have someone for all departments and the business continues to tick along without me.

This is not easy to set up and create – it takes time but the investment in a team is worth your sanity and time abundance. You can always make more money but you cannot buy more time. Time is a finite resource we all get given and don't know exactly when it will run out. And because of this, setting things up for you to have more time is key for you to make the most of your time on this earth.

CHAPTER 35

LEVERAGEABLE INVESTMENT OPTIONS

Depending on your age and capacity, what you invest in and how much will differ from person to person. That's why in the upcoming chapters I will talk about a variety of places and options I have explored and why. These won't be all the options available out there, I just don't feel I can write about something I have never done. That has always been my style. I only share what it is I have taken action on, risked and how it has turned out. Even in my business, I do not teach my authors anything I have not done myself. I think that is inauthentic and deceiving. I believe in walking my talk and I will leave other strategies to other writers that have played in those arenas.

One thing I do know is that if something sounds too good to be true, it usually is. The promise of get rich quick or taking uneducated shots at investments has never worked out for me. Trust me I have made three pretty expensive decisions in the hope for quick passive income. I will talk through each of them here so that you can start to get a feel for what it may look like if you come across it.

Investment Mistake #1 – This goes way back before business ownership, just after the Thailand holiday with my mum and Stuart in 2006. I had read *Rich Dad Poor Dad* and all of a sudden realised that I should be investing in assets and not liabilities or keeping my cash in the back. We had some saved funds and as we were focusing on looking to invest in one of the strategies Robert Kiyosaki was talking about which was shares. So an email happened to come to us from that old poor accountant I told you about earlier. We went to a presentation with my mum and I was very convinced that we should both put in $5000 each. We did and watched that money go up and down for a while. Don't ask me what we were funding

PART 3: PROFIT TO FREEDOM

with this money as I didn't know anything about shares or how it all works. WARNING!!! If you know nothing, do not go in blind and uninformed or uneducated. Eventually as far as I remember that company liquidated and we never saw a cent of our money. At the time as employees earning 50K a year that was huge money for us and my mum.

Investment Mistake #2 – Back in 2010/11 when I trying to get my coaching business off the ground, I invested a lot in courses, mentors, programs ... I was trying anything to see how I can start monetising something. In that time I came across a Sydney one-day seminar (aka as 'Pitch Fest') and one of the people presenting was a guy from a company Speedlings – it was all about this super easy way a system would build you a website and then magically companies that advertise on your website will pay you affiliate commissions for showing their ads. The guy even demoed live in his talk a brand-new website build and money suddenly started ticking over. It seems so easy and fast – WARNING!!! That should have been my sign but just like all other excited people there, I ran up to the tables and signed up ... 12 months later with all action followed and implemented nothing – not a cent and no honour of their 12-month money back guarantee if you did all the work. They turned out to be a scam and 20K went down the drain to oblivion. That was huge money for me at the time that I didn't have.

Investment Mistake #3 – This one is recent, from 2022. It didn't hurt as much as what I invested didn't make a dent in my savings at all but it was still 20K from my end and once again I encouraged my mum to join in and she trusts me wholeheartedly, so she put in around 3K too. I was told about this investment opportunity from one of my team members and I did as much learning about it as I could before I took the leap. It seemed legit and I met someone that was already making great money for a few years through it. It was to do with currency exchange trading but the company CashFx was doing it on your behalf and each Sunday you got a really regular distribution from which you can reinvest and keep growing your portfolio to a point when it reaches 100K, and you were set to make around $2800 USD a week ongoing. For six months I saw mine receive regular distributions and growth and at three months Mum joined as she watched it grow. So was my teammate. Then all of a sudden the systems started changing, they were going to bring out a debit card so you can use your money easier and the distributions dried up and then completely stopped. No further communication and to this day I don't know what has happened to that money – I just assume it is gone. I have better things to do with my time than dwell on my poor decision. WARNING!!! If it sounds too good to be true, it most likely is. And this definitely was that. It was also connected to cryptocurrency which I don't understand at all so that should have been another big warning – do not go in uneducated!

I do not blame my teammate for telling me about this opportunity as she experienced a similar if not greater loss. I made the decision and I live with each of my decisions – good or bad without blame. Onwards and upwards! I know I am going to make back that money 1000-fold moving forward.

This hasn't stopped me from investing. The difference is that nowadays I ask for advice from my financial independence team, do deeper due diligence and go for the more well-known slow and steady strategies that I will talk about in the upcoming chapters. I know there will be more flops in the future and places where I will lose but I also know that I will be able to minimise them from what I now know from experience. If you never take any risks you will never grow or learn. I know for a fact my investments have been skewed more heavily on the positive growing side than the loss side. In fact, the above are a drop in the ocean to what we have built in terms of our net worth through the investments we are going to go through next.

PART 3: PROFIT TO FREEDOM

CHAPTER 36

TOTAL BUSINESS FREEDOM

This chapter covers an investment, not of money, but of time. You and your team's time to build a business that you 'grow to exit'. You won't live forever and neither will your business, unless one of your children wants to take it over or you end up selling it to someone that would love to have something established and with an awesome reputation, database and clientele.

You never know what will happen, how long you will want to run your business and in fact we have covered so far that ultimately the goal is for your business not to be owner reliant. That is why investing time in writing and documenting all your systems is key to replacing yourself out of every role as well as having your asset 'exit and handover ready' when the time comes. Starting on this sooner rather than later is a great way to build the habit in system creation and you will thank yourself and your team for it as when someone leaves and someone else comes in they will not need as much training as all the systems will be there for them to follow.

So it's not only great to build systems to sell the business, it is also a wonderful resource for onboarding new team members and ramping them up faster. It's really useful when someone goes away on holidays or is on leave too, as others can more easily take over their role without too much disruption to the day-to-day running of the business.

I will not be teaching you how to go about it in this short chapter, but I have a book to recommend, *Systemology* by David Jenyns. I read it and then my team's systems champion read it and we have been busy breaking everything down and completing our systems. We gave ourselves a year to go over them fully and then we will be updating them and adding to them as things change and we add in more tasks. We have gotten in the habit as soon as we notice a process we are doing the we haven't written up to immediately write it while it is fresh in our head when we have just completed it.

Take our return to live events recently. I had a four-and-a-half year pause when I went fully online, and now I am back in the physical event space. Things are different to five years ago and I didn't even have systems then. We are doing it all over again and as I get each one finished we are adding and editing what we are doing until we arrive at our new seamless formula for them.

If I ever need to tell someone how to do something I record a screenshare and add it to the systems. Each Monday at our team meeting we report what we have created and our systems champion gives us the next lot of systems to create. Each one of us does one hour a week on this – as there are seven of us, that is seven hours of systems writing that gets done. I have no doubt we will smash it out by the end of this year. What a wonderful investment, as I can then ask a business broker to evaluate our business and see where we are sitting. At exit, I know I will be celebrating big time!

CHAPTER 37

REAL ESTATE ABUNDANCE

I bought my first property at the age of 25. It was a one-bedroom flat. My stepdad Dennis was always big on getting into the market as soon as possible and always said how important it was to also pay it down as quickly as possible. He had worked really hard to pay off his first property in his twenties while his friends partied and always made decisions based on valuing, buying, selling or renting properties. In fact, he decided to retire during the pandemic and move up north to Queensland when he turned 60. He and my mum were together for 20 years and we all still talk. He never owned a business and the way he set himself up for a comfortable retirement was through having a few properties fully paid off, downsizing and moving to a warmer climate and a cheaper lifestyle location.

From this type of influence during my teenage years, as I moved to Australia at the age of 14, I also knew to value real estate and investing for the long term. I sold the first flat as it was in partnership with a boyfriend prior to meeting my husband. My mum took over for him and paid him out and from the sale profits (which we split with Mum) I bought the first house with my husband Stuart when we were 28. We lived there till we had our first child Judd and then upsized to our second house without selling the first as my father-in-law moved into it and we got to keep it.

The second and then third baby followed and we needed to upsize again ... so, we did and kept the second house. At this stage the business could support the new mortgage and we were earning rent that was maintaining the second. We paid off the first house loan as it ended up seeming tiny seven years on. That house still has my father-in-law living in it with no income coming from it – however it is fully paid off and has quadrupled in value since we bought it now 19 years ago.

After our third home, the business was growing and maintaining consistently, and we had great equity from the three properties so we continued investing each year into more real estate. We built a brand-new dual occupancy in Albury that brings two rental incomes, we got a great capital growth property in Langwarrin, Melbourne, we paid off our big primary home, we invested in Perth and Rockhampton, and last year I took the leap into our first commercial property in Toowoomba. Currently we are working on a NDIS special new build home for people with disability. This will be fantastic positive cashflow (high yield). We also added an extra massive bedroom for my son in our primary home and increased its value further last Christmas.

During the pandemic, when we had our first long four-month lockdown, I had this brilliant idea. As two of our homes were paid off, nothing was really being offset by what I call our big account where we keep our buffer funds. So, we got a house on the Gold Coast. After four years this home has not cost us anything as it is fully offset (so no interest payments) and hasn't earned us anything as we just use it for our own private use when we like. I spend around three months at that home each year. We escaped quite a few lockdowns up there. Yes, we can earn a lot from this property, but there isn't a need at this moment and this house has gone up 400K + in value since we bought it. I host my team for annual conferences there and we have done quite a bit of renovations and improvements over the four years that help with the value of the home.

As you can tell, I love this strategy. Once again, it's not a get rich quick process. I've been in this game for 22 years now and build in a slow, steady and methodical way. It has helped having a profitable business so that I can pay things down quicker than being on a set income. This is how we have arrived at financial independence.

There are many different methods to succeed with real estate. I am super blessed to have a great team around me that has advised me on some of the purchases, helped in the set-up of mortgages and I've utilised a few buyers' agents for some of our properties to save time and ultimately make more money by making the right choices. Where can you start today? Is there something you can do in your primary home to instil more equity in it? Have you sussed out with a broker what kind of borrowing power you have? What are your financial independence goals and how can investing in real estate get you closer to them?

PART 3: PROFIT TO FREEDOM

If you are in your twenties, thirties or even forties you have the luxury of time to play its part that real estate needs. That's not to say you can't do it in your fifties or sixties as well. I have met quite a few clever real estate investors that only started five years ago and with particular strategies built an amazing portfolio and reached their goals. It's all possible – the question is are you willing to do what it takes to hit your goals?

CHAPTER 38

BOUNTIFUL BONDS

My financial advisor suggested we get some as a tax saving strategy due to our high-income nature. I don't have the full language around it but here is what I looked up on Chat GPT as to what bonds are:

In financial terms, bonds are debt securities issued by entities such as governments, municipalities or corporations to raise capital. When you purchase a bond, you are essentially lending money to the issuer in exchange for periodic interest payments and the return of the bond's face value when it matures.

Here's a breakdown of key bond components:

1. Issuer: The entity that issues the bond and borrows the funds.
2. Principal (face value): The amount of money the bondholder will receive back when the bond matures.
3. Coupon rate: The interest rate that the bond issuer will pay to the bondholder. This is usually paid semi-annually.
4. Maturity date: The date when the bond issuer must repay the principal to the bondholder.

5. Yield: The return a bondholder gets on the bond, typically expressed as an annual percentage. This can be affected by the bond's price and interest rates.

Bonds are generally considered safer investments compared to stocks, as they typically provide fixed interest payments and return of principal, though they still carry risks such as default risk (issuer failing to repay) and interest rate risk (changes in interest rates affecting bond prices).

High-income earner: A high-income earner might invest in municipal bonds to reduce their taxable interest income since the interest from municipal bonds is tax-exempt at the federal level.

That being said, we invest each and every month in these. We even have another set up for our children that I will talk about in a later chapter. We set this up from the day our first child was born.

I would speak to someone that knows more about these and see if they are the right fit for your investment strategy. By having this as set and forget at our end we have another nest egg of funds that is growing steadily month after month. We get annual updates on the growth and total from our advisor. She reviews our risk profiles and invests in appropriate things matched up to our risk profile.

CHAPTER 39

SENSATIONAL SUPER

Those that earn a regular wage, have superannuation deducted automatically from their wages and they don't need to think about putting it aside. When you become a business owner no-one pays your superannuation, and you must willingly choose to contribute to it each year.

It's tough at the start of your business as you may not have the spare funds to put into super, as anything spare you end up using to build the business. But there will come a time as you grow to be profitable and a high earner that you must be clever and invest some of your money into super. I remember my accountant and financial advisor banging on about this for years to me. I didn't listen for two or three years, but then I changed my thinking and started putting in the maximum allowed super contribution for me and my husband. See, at high-income you could be paying 45% tax on your earnings whereas when you put it in super, it is only taxed at 15% and at retirement you can withdraw it tax free.

I have set ours up on monthly direct debits from my account so it's set and forget and I don't have to come up with a lump sum during June each year. This way I don't feel it as much and it gets done. Another nest egg that is growing as time passes. We have caught up significantly on the missed years and the best bit is that you are also able to buy a property through your super, so that may be something we explore in the future.

The mindset around super needs to be similar to holding onto real estate. You are holding and investing your funds that will hopefully grow over time for your future financial comfort. Yes, super is invested into stocks so as the market goes up and down, so will your super balance. If you are younger, they advise to go into high-risk high reward set up, then as you get older and you may need access to it, your set up may involve low risk and lower rewards scenarios. Talk to your accountant and/or financial advisor for your specific circumstance.

CHAPTER 40

CASH FOR KICKS

Bottom line is, if you don't have it, don't spend it on liabilities. Cash is king in this instance and in fact in every instance aside from borrowing to buy assets and build your wealth.

Last year we replaced our two cars. One I bought cash and the other we paid partially cash and partially a car loan that I was told we could pay out sooner without penalty. I don't know why I did that as I had the money. I just thought if I pay 5-10K over the year it won't feel like a lump sum. Until the time came when I thought I had paid it off and then more monthly instalments kept coming out. WTF! I tried to phone the company but unfortunately they were really bad at their customer service and for months I was being handballed to someone else.

It was so frustrating and we paid more to get out of the loan. There was apparently interest that you have to pay at the back end of the loan that I had no idea was a thing. Not only did this car end up costing us 3-4K more than the purchase price but with months of chasing the company and phone calls it was most likely more like 10K in my time and sanity I wasted trying to do it that way. This is the time I decided I will never ever buy cars on a loan again – unless I plan to have that loan over the five to seven years it is set.

If you have the cash use it. Another thing is credit cards. I use mine to pay for absolutely everything as we get our Qantas frequent flyer points and they provide us with that one fully paid all-inclusive trip with my husband Stuart every single year. Recently I booked a $135 one-way flight, Los Angeles to Melbourne for our family of six using points and pay, saving over $5000. However, I never owe anything on the credit card. I check it pretty much daily and pay it out weekly. No credit card crazy interest rates for me – no thank you! The banks hate people like me as we know how to work the system, use the perks and don't give them anything more.

Same thing goes when on holidays. We never buy trips or use spending money we don't have. If I don't have it, I don't spend it – it's as simple as that.

Always ask lots of questions when it comes to loans, as the lenders will only tell you the easy and straightforward stuff to get you through and make the sale. Always compare companies, and another option could be to refinance your home loan as the interest rate on those is much lower than credit cards or car loans.

Sometimes when you are starting out, you may need to buy some things on credit card, but always be of the mindset to pay things down quickly and not dip into it over and over. Keeping all this under control can be a challenge for different personalities, so my advice is to either get help, set some ground rules up, have an accountability buddy and don't make buying decision by yourself if you have the tendency to be spontaneous and worry about it later.

Even nowadays we track our cashflow. If we feel our sales are on the lower side, we tighten our belts for a little while and ride it out and when its abundant we feel that we can spend or invest a bit more. Money management is key to sustainable wealth and growth of your money tree in life.

CHAPTER 41

TRAVEL NOW!!! MAKING TIME FOR MINI RETIREMENTS

The time to enjoy life and all it has to offer is while you have the energy and stamina to do it. Waiting for retirement age of 65 or even older now is a big gamble. How do you even know you will be around to see 65? We don't know what's around the corner and we must enjoy our present. We also don't know what our health status will be as we age.

In my first year of business, I read the *4-Hour Work Week* book and the author talked about having mini retirements. I absolutely love this and I also think it's the key to longevity in business, boosting our creativity and avoidance of burnout. I know that the first three to five years it can feel intense and super busy. Working night and day, weekends, public holidays, pretty much what feels like 24/7. But I also know that too shall pass and you must be smart when it does.

We talked about your 'enough' number earlier and using this you will know when you are at a level you would like to sustain what you do. With each passing year, hopefully you have systemised and outsourced your business tasks and roles and the business is less and less business owner reliant. It is time to block out your calendar. The very first thing that I do in mine is block out my mini retirements. I generally know I will be off most of December and January due to summer and school holidays here in Australia and around the other school holidays throughout the year. My husband and I block out our week away and a couple of other long weekend trips we like to take alone.

I may be going away just with mum – so I block that out too and then there may be trips with girlfriends or fun retreats with my clients which feel like holidays anyway. Once all that is in (approximately taking up four months out of the 12) I start working on all my other business events and activities.

Having something to look forward to is really important. This year for the first time I took out annual travel insurance for the family as you save money and we need it all the time. Each time we travel we would be taking it out the night before and splitting it up is time consuming as well as more expensive.

I can't stress enough the importance that time off to explore the world has on your continued success. When you get away from your everyday routine, you start to see things differently and as your brain has a chance to go out to pasture, it resets. Random spontaneous ideas manifest from doing nothing. There is also this feeling I get on the way home of excitement to get back into things, see my clients and return to my 'at home' routine.

Booking ahead of time (we usually have things booked 12–18 months in advance) saves time and money in the long run. Flights are cheaper, you can find great accommodation deals (we love Luxury Escapes) and you know all that you are looking forward to and can make a great plan of what to do when you get there. As we run an events business, for us this is a must to know our calendar that much time in advance. People want notice and events need pre-planning and organisation that you cannot do last minute.

Travelling while you are young or with young children enables you to use the knowledge you gain in what you do. Your kids end up being comfortable in brand-new surroundings and cultures. They learn so much more through experiencing than from simply going to school. As they watch you problem-solve as you travel, you are demonstrating a key life skill they will need. The best bit is, you end up having so many wonderful memories of your experiences together that you talk about for life.

I would have to say travel is my largest spend in my life. I value experiences and memories more than having a super fancy home or car. I like nice things, I just like to go to and see nice places a lot more. We don't remember what we got for Christmas last year, but we never forget the trips we took with the people we love.

TRAVEL NOW!!! While you are young. And take those mini-retirements!

CHAPTER 42

RICH KIDS

It may be too late for this for some of you reading this book, but I am hoping this book will also be picked up by those a bit younger too that are planning a family or about to have a baby. After all, I was the person that picked up a cassette tape from Robert Kiyosaki, author of *Rich Dad Poor Dad* alongside his books called *The Cashflow Game* and this cassette shared how your child can become a billionaire. I was 29 at the time.

What was shared was very simple. Set aside $100 each month for your child from the day they are born and keep going having it invested say in something that returns 8% and with the power of compound interest this will eventuate into $1B by the time that child is 65. I know this is a huge time frame and highly unlikely someone would do it for this long, however the idea of doing something consistently for your children is key. I started this when my first child Judd was born and added on more for my second and third children as they were born. It is all set and forget so I don't need to think about putting it aside.

I recently doubled my investment from $300 a month to $600 as we would like to help our children in some way but not a way that would mean finding funds or dipping into money intended for something else. At the time of writing this pot has grown to $60K and gaining more and more momentum. Set and forget is such a powerful way or making what you have left over fit your lifestyle. I understand sometimes it feels like you cannot spare anything. I remember I was not a business owner when my first child was born and when he was 18 months old, my husband lost a business we had so we went backwards. I didn't stop the $100 a month – $25 a week was my commitment to my child's future. I just went without other things instead.

I set and forget superannuation, other bonds, regular investments and even my mum's weekly wage as I know without me she would not be able to support herself. It is never too late to start saving or putting things on set and forget. This was the way I paid down our home loan too – I just put $1000 a week to go on the home loan on top of what the bank was taking. Time plays its part for the rest. That is why it's so important to budget and know your numbers. At certain times of the year it can be quite heavy on expenses and others full of abundance. It all evens out at the end of the day.

Start small and build on that. The numbers I am sharing were not that big when I started doing it – $25 a week was where I started. You can too!!!

CHAPTER 43

ACCUMULATE THEN LIQUIDATE

We come into this world with nothing and we definitely leave with nothing. Just like a bell curve we grow, grow and grow until we reach our 'enough' stage and then slowly begin to downsize and simplify so that we can enjoy our golden years free of stuff, stress and responsibilities. As you build your business, it is key that you are investing your profits in asset building vehicles and holding on as time does its magic in terms of capital growth.

Your business will also grow, so make sure you have your systems documented and it will become a great asset that you can sell at exit. When we are young we have the capacity to manage lots of different projects, people and problems. You get tired of that stuff later on, and you want less on your plate.

Every year in our home we complete a mission declutter and get rid of things no longer adding value to our lives. Every year, I donate or trash more and more. In fact, my goal is to only have less than 50% capacity used in all my storage spaces and when I am an empty nester to just get down to bare minimum.

I don't know what is going to happen but one of my money mentors explained this cycle to me that we go through in life. I can see how it will unfold, I just don't know when. Currently I think I still have a good 10 years in the accumulation stage with our assets and who knows maybe one of my children may like to take over the business and perhaps we will maintain some of our properties to live off rent our tenants pay.

I guess that is the next book. I cannot write about it until I have been through it myself, but that is the idea. I don't see myself just chilling or being a couch potato. There will be projects on the go and I can't wait to see what that future brings as our best work is always ahead of us.

PART 4

MILLIONAIRE AUTHORS

The time has come to highlight some of my amazing millionaire authors that have also upleveled their lives and businesses through writing books. Their stories are quite different, but I am sure you will agree that the mindset behind how they used their books is quite similar.

I know for a fact that I was not the only one responsible in helping them achieve their success. Their success is due to their commitment, hard work and determination to do what most others won't. They have invested huge amounts of money as I have in mentors and programs to grow personally and professionally. I am just a little chuffed that I played a small part in their journey to success and have absolutely loved watching their growth and expansion to bigger and better things.

Eleni Mitas did my second retreat back in February 2014, Rachael Evans, my sixth retreat in Feb 2015, Francesca Moi, my ninth retreat in Nov 2015 and Diane McKendrick, my 22nd retreat in August 2018. Seeing these inspirational women grow, pivot and take on the world by going international with their business has been the most wonderful gift I can ever get back for what I do. Let's hear what they have to say...

CHAPTER 44

DIANE MCKENDRICK – GET MORE BANG FOR YOUR BOOK

My name is Diane McKendrick, fondly referred to by my peers as Millionaire Mum.

Together with my older sister, Michelle Anne, we are known as Those2Sisters, and we show businesswomen around the world how to drop from their head to their heart and listen to their whispers so that they can cut the crap, do the thing, and be the woman they were born to be.

Can you hear your whisper right now as you read or listen to this chapter? I guarantee it is whispering something to you right now. Most of us are too busy being busy to hear it, distracted by doing.

If you listen closely enough, you might hear your whisper saying things like, *write the book, start the podcast, create the online course, reach out to that person, go to the retreat, stop drinking coffee, give up the 5 pm wine, take the leap, do the thing ...*

And, of course, it will be met with what I call the wounding. Typically, the voice of your wounding is louder and clearer, and it will obnoxiously loop, saying things like, *you're too dumb to do that, no-one will read or listen to it, you don't know how, you can't afford that, why are you sitting here reading when you should be doing laundry, prepping dinner, or one of the other hundred things we do around the house ...*

Your whisper is the word we use for intuition or divine guidance, and your wounding is your trauma or the narrative and story you are telling yourself to keep you small and safe. It has an important role, certainly not to be dismissed, but definitely needs to be managed – especially for those of you who are ready to get more bang for your book, create wealth and freedom, and use your book as the cornerstone to your next level of activation in life and business.

A quick trip down memory lane so you can gauge who I am, what my journey has been, and why the heck you should listen to me when there is an overwhelming amount of content, education and experts out there in the personal development industry telling you all how to make more money, do more, be more!

Let's face it – these days, it's easy to get fixated, frustrated, distracted and lose heart and momentum pretty quickly if you listen to everyone.

My first and upfront invitation is to read the first few paragraphs of my chapter and decide if you resonate with me personally ... and if your whisper says, 'I like her, keep reading', trust yourself and keep reading!

And if it says, 'nah, not for me', trust your whisper and move on to the next author or chapter. I won't be offended.

Your time is precious, and it is my intention that through my chapter, I can offer valuable and insightful information on how I went from a shy, timid, small-town girl with a big dream and no idea, to a Millionaire Mum living the best of both worlds with the support of my books and ongoing mentoring from Natasa Denman and her team.

There are plenty of beautiful women in this book who are also close friends of mine and super successful. The beauty is, we do life and business very differently. The similar thread that weaves us all together is a willingness to cheer for and support each other and a deep commitment to service, legacy and impact. A commitment to our communities to continue to show up, fall down, and get back up again. No matter how hard it gets.

Another brief reminder before I dive deeper into my personal journey and practical tips on getting more bang for your book ... there will be hard times.

As Natasa calls them, 'shit hits the fan moments', and I had to learn the hard way how to prepare and be present with these as my business boomed, then bombed, and then boomed again ... and surely at some point may bomb again. The difference this time is that I have systems, structures and strategies in place to support the rapid growth and the cyclical nature of business in unprecedented times. I am more deeply attuned to my whisper, which certainly makes for a smoother ride.

Once again, being able to discern and relate differently to your whisper and wounding will support you through tough times and give you guidance you can't buy at the shops or read about in a book.

Through this chapter, I will share with authenticity and transparency my behind-the-scenes journey of becoming a four-time bestselling author. How I achieved my current lifestyle, identity and freedom in alignment with my values and not at the sacrifice of them.

Which is something I had to learn the hard way after burning out as a new business owner trying to do it all. A rite of passage, an initiation, which once again I was warned about, but being a visionary, I kept going full steam ahead. Until I hit that brick wall.

Since I was a little girl, I had a dream to become an author, and the voice of my wounding had a field day with it – looping loudly, it offered all the excuses: *I have no idea how and I can't spell, I don't know how, people like me don't do things like that. Who am I to write a book? I'm an imposter or fraud, I'm scared, what will people say, no-one will read it, what if I make a spelling mistake …?* And the list goes on!

In 2018, I met Natasa, and the opportunity slapped me in the face. For one of the first times in my life, my whisper became louder: *Do it, find a way.* But the voice of my wounding also got louder and double-time, looping loudly again.

Keeping me stuck, *I can't afford it, I don't have time*, and I certainly didn't have the confidence. I was a stay-at-home mum with two kids, and my husband was an international airline pilot. Still up breastfeeding at nights and operating on very little sleep.

With my wounding going to town, I signed the dotted line with Nat. I was terrified!

My body was physically shaking, my breath short and sharp. I had two weeks to prepare for the 48-Hour Writers' Retreat, find a babysitter, leave my young children. I didn't sleep properly for two weeks before the retreat, and when the retreat arrived, I had so much fear my body responded with chronic pain. My neck and back jammed for the duration of the retreat.

Using the technique I now teach in my world-class retreats and sold-out online courses, I resourced myself, and by some miracle (and Nat and the team's support and streamlined process), my first book, *Rise Up: The Soulful Guide to Success*, was published and became a bestseller three months later.

The wounding kicked in again shortly after, and I could hear the battle and conflict in my mind. How can I sell enough books to get my return on investment? I had already crunched the numbers and realised it was going to take selling a LOT of books at $30 to pay off the publishing package, let alone make my first million.

And the truth is, I had little to no following or anyone that actually wanted to buy my book (apart from my family and the ladies in my mother's group and the other mums at the kids' swimming lessons).

So to be honest, I was gutted. I felt like a failure, a fraud.

The pressure was on as COVID had hit, and my husband lost his job overnight. One of our 'shit hits the fan moments'. Our family went into crisis mode, and it was one of the hardest times of our lives, wondering if we could stay in our home, how we would pay for our groceries, feed and clothe our kids. I had spent all this money on my dream of writing a book and felt selfish and like a fool.

My first book was not the cash cow I thought it would be, and I felt like it was my fault our family was falling apart and we were in a financial crisis.

As the days passed by and the hole seemed to get deeper and darker, I started to get curious and change my perspective. Something enlightening about hitting rock bottom. I had great mentors, friends and family around me.

One day, as I was journalling, I remembered Nat saying to us, 'It's not about the book; it's about the person you become writing it.'

I started to review my notes from her webinars and trainings and remembered her comment about 'your book becomes your business card on steroids'.

So I got to work (with the words of Nat's mum Bubzi ringing in my ears, 'every beginning is hard').

I attuned to my whispers, met my wounding head-on, and I started creating.

I started using my first book as my business card on steroids.

I recorded it as an audiobook so I could use it as a lead magnet, and within months, with extra coaching from Francesca Moi at the time, I got fully booked one-on-one with clients. She taught me about relationships, funnels and supported me in learning about business.

With the support of my two mentors, Natasa Denman and Francesca Moi, and my first book by my side, I took massive, rapid and inspired action.

I modelled their business structure and started half-day workshops based on my first book, *Rise Up: The Soulful Guide to Success*.

My first half-day workshop was called '6 Steps to Soulful Success'. All attendees got a copy of my book, and these events started to sell out. I was nervous and unsure but kept putting one foot in front of the other.

In my half-days, people were deeply moved and inspired by my story and wanted more from me, so I created a retreat. I still had no money, so I bought a lotus bell tent and ran them in my backyard. At $500 a pop, totally undercharging people, and costing me $$$.

My whisper said, 'keep going'. So I did. I did everything at these retreats: cooking, cleaning, delivering, sales, preparation. EVERYTHING.

People read or listened to my book, and they changed from the core. Pure transformation for women because of what I had created. Changed forever from the inside out. I started to receive calls from ladies' husbands saying, 'Thank you, I don't know what you did to her, but I got the woman I married back.'

My clients (and their husbands) wanted more, so I attuned to my whisper and created a podcast, once again using the book as the anchor. Season 1, of the 'Rise and Shine Podcast Series' was born. This took a lot of courage, as even my coach at the time suggested not to do the podcast as I had already taken on so much. Concerned I would burn out, she advised against it.

I didn't listen to my coach because my whisper was louder. I didn't tell her; I just did it. This is your call forward that if you are working with a coach, make sure you attune to the voice of your whisper and not outsource that decision to someone else. Even the best coach in the world won't trump YOUR whisper.

Now I am up to nearly 200 episodes and created an online product to help other authors plan, produce, and publish their podcasts – to date, that product has supported over 30 women globally to get their voice out to the world.

The podcast has grown with the addition of each book. Now up to Season 3, it is called 'The Aligned Woman's Way' (my third book, which I will share with you later).

BOOK SALES WON'T MAKE YOU RICH

Getting the podcast set up and running took longer than it should have as I am tech challenged. I literally sat and asked Google questions and took one step at a time.

People wanted more, so the next natural progression for me was to expand into packaging it ALL together.

I created 'Rise and Shine' packages. Natasa and Francesca charged $10K–$20K, so I thought, if they can do it, so can I. A bit of a bold move considering to this point the most I had charged was $500 for a three-day retreat. The central nervous system struggled with this one, once again. As well as listening and being guided by my whisper, I simply opened my book and consumed my own content. To take the leap and get it done.

So I did it. I said to my sister a few days before my one online half-day, 'I'm going to sell a $10K package today' and she said, 'You can't do that; you don't have one.'

My response when someone tells me, 'You can't do that'? I simply ask, 'Why not?' And if I listen to the answer from my wounding, I'll sit around procrastinating, make excuses, get distracted. Alternatively, when I attune to my whisper ...

I sold five, paid in full that day. I want to remind you here: 'It's not about the book; it's about the person you become and the launch pad it provides you to leap from.'

Granted, I didn't actually have an official package, but I had a whole heap of products which I could package up, and I remember both Nat and Francesca told me, 'Sell it, then create it.' So, I did. I had no systems, no team, no structure, no invoices, but I had written a book and attuned to my whisper, so I just followed the next cue. Packaged my products with my book as the core ...

Over time, $10K packages turned into $15K packages, $30K, $50K, and maybe one day soon, even more.

Okay, team – if you're still with me reading this chapter, I feel like I'm on fast forward here, and contributing this chapter in Nat's book is giving me a reality check of what I have actually accomplished as a result of listening to my whisper and writing my first book. But wait, there is MORE – a lot MORE!

I started to post photos of my sold-out events and retreats. And the next thing on my list to get credibility was to get on stage. Go one to many. Get my message out to more people.

I listened to my whisper again. I overheard someone talk about Crowd Pleaser, which is a free platform to match event coordinators with speakers. She whispered, 'Set it up, NOW'.

I excused myself from the conversation I was in and set it up immediately. I didn't have professional photos but used photos of me holding my book in front of Nat and Francesca's community. Also, something to note here is that I'm tech challenged, and it took me half a day to do a 20-minute job of getting my Crowd Pleaser profile up. Here is your cue: if you're a fellow author and reading this, keen to get on stages, go set it up NOW!

I started to get speaking gigs. I did them for free at first, taking my books, selling them, giving them away, sharing my journey. My feed started to fill with photos of me on stages everywhere.

And then … It happened. I felt that awful feeling in my tummy as the whisper said, 'Di, it's time to charge'. So I fumbled my way through Crowd Pleaser and put a $300 price tag on a 30-minute talk. I was sweating, terrified, felt like a fraud … then I forgot about it. Until a little over one month later, SOMEONE BOOKED ME.

OMG, friends – I nearly fell off my chair. I quoted someone $300, and they said YES!!!! And then $500, and then $2000, and now up to $6000.

TO SPEAK!!!

To stand on stage and make people laugh, cry, snap them off autopilot, and see what else is out there for them. I started to get invited to speak internationally.

A dream come true.

Money started to flow in, things got easy, and my business skyrocketed – not quite yet to the million mark, but it was on track.

Life was good.

And then … COVID craziness really hit. The lockdowns, the vaccinations, the uncertainty.

And the hard truth set in again.

My business, with the support of my husband, had quadrupled his income as an international airline pilot. At home during school hours from our garage. I was still available for school pick-ups, drop-offs, and singing them bedtime stories.

It was during this time my second book was birthed, *Millionaire Mum: The Best of Both Worlds*.

We were stuck at home, my business was not yet a million-dollar business but had the potential. This book took seven months because I had so much fear or wounding telling me, *It's not true, you're a liar, you're not a millionaire* ... I also had my whisper guiding me, *This book is a declaration to the universe that this is the path for me. Boldly claiming my identity in this industry as both millionaire and mum and showing other mums how to do it too.*

Once again, book sales were disappointing. I remember times being at events standing at my table, proud as punch with not one but two bestselling books, and there would be one or two people at my table while the lady beside me had 20 people deep in her line to buy her book. Gutted, I went home and started asking questions again.

Reminded of the harsh truth that it is not about the book, I tuned in again to see what products could be developed from the core of the book as an addition to or extension of ...

And then my Fit Family protein range was birthed.

My Heart 2 Heart Cacao brand brought to life.

My sports clothing line.

My Ascension range of sterling silver jewellery.

Bookmarks.

Pixie Affirmation Card Deck.

I upgraded my retreats and refused to cancel any during the crazy COVID times. In fact, after my second book and the new identity I unleashed, I added a new retreat (while everyone else was cancelling theirs). We called it 'The Energetics of Business Retreat' and took business ladies up to a luxurious location at Port Douglas. It was smack bang in the middle of COVID, and everyone was telling me, 'You can't do that, what if there is a lockdown?'

By some miracle, it was nestled in between lockdowns by days on each side. I oversold the retreat and ended up having to get two houses. We all masked up, jumped on the plane, and somehow had the most moving, transformational, powerful and potent time away.

From here, we created our highest-end package, 'Energetics of Business Mastermind', which we run every six months for high-end businesswomen who come together from all over the world to coach in our container and have access to the massive, powerful and conscious community we have crafted from the ground up.

Luckily, by this stage, the business was booming as a result of my books. My sister had gotten the sack from the police force after 25 years for not being vaccinated, so she joined my business full-time, and we became Those2Sisters.

She is now in the business as the COO, and I am the CEO of Those2Sisters Pty Ltd. We have a team of three virtual assistants. Thanks to Michelle Anne, my older sister, who is outcome-focused, organised and an overall powerhouse woman, our business runs smoothly in the back end, while I stay in creation mode and she works her magic.

PART 4: MILLIONAIRE AUTHORS

By the time I was ready to write my third book, I thought people might have heard enough about me, so I decided to sell the chapters out to my clients as co-authors and get their authoring journey started.

Seven co-authors, including my sister Michelle Anne, said yes, and this has been one of my most fulfilling accomplishments to date. To mentor my blood sister and soul sister clients to become bestselling authors and witness their transformation within the pages of my third bestselling book.

This book is called *The Aligned Woman's Way: For Women Slaying in Business at the Sacrifice of Themselves* and became the cornerstone of our signature online course, 'The Aligned Woman Academy'.

I am finally at the end of this chapter, and my wounding is telling me I talked about myself waaaaayyy too much. I don't usually share my accomplishments because they become my new normal very quickly, and to be honest, I focus on the present moment and what I am creating and cultivating for my community NOW.

I trust that by sharing what is possible by being guided by your whisper and writing your first book, I will inspire you to take the next step wherever you are at in your journey. TRUST yourself and remember, it's not about the how; it's about the NOW and which voice you choose to listen to.

All my love,
Diane

CHAPTER 45

ELENI MITAS –THE POWER OF MINDSET DOMINANCE: FROM LOUNGE ROOM TO GLOBAL HYPNOTHERAPY LEADER

In May 2010, I embarked on a journey that would transform my life and career in unimaginable ways. Having left my full-time employment as an economist and completed my qualifications as a hypnotherapist, I started seeing clients in my lounge room. My goal was simple yet ambitious: to create a successful six-figure business that could replace my corporate income. With a large mortgage and the responsibility of covering half of it, failure was not an option. Little did I know, this journey would eventually lead me to create a seven-figure business, a rare feat in the hypnotherapy profession where most practitioners still needed a second job to make ends meet.

A synchronous meeting with Natasa Denman

In 2012, a pivotal moment occurred when I attended a networking event and met Natasa Denman. Natasa, who was a weight loss coach at the time, was sitting at my table. I was immediately impressed by her achievements; she had licensed her coaching business overseas, and her husband Stuart had quit his job to support her full-time. This level of success was exactly what I aspired to achieve for my own business.

Natasa soon started her book coaching business, and her words about having a book being like 'a business card on steroids' resonated deeply with me. I knew that writing a book could propel my business forward, especially in breaking into the corporate market where I aimed to secure speaking engagements. At that time, I was already seeing a significant number of clients each week, thanks to my massive action-taking approach and the Universe delivering clients my way.

The birth of 'mindset dominance'

With a schedule packed with 25 clients a week, I realised I needed accountability to complete my book. Without it, I knew it would never get done. So, I decided to attend Natasa's Ultimate 48 Hour Author Retreat.

Initially, I titled my book *Mindset Dominance: Fit and Energised in 90 Days. A Blueprint for the Busy Executive,* targeting corporate executives who needed a mental and physical boost.

The decision to write this book was one of the best I ever made. Upon its publication, I pitched a one-day workshop to a business and secured the gig. However, as I continued to grow my hypnotherapy practice, I realised that I wanted my book to serve a broader purpose. Thus, I rebranded it to *Mindset Dominance: Stop Self Sabotage and Break Bad Habits* in its second edition.

The journey to global recognition

Publishing *Mindset Dominance* opened numerous doors for me. It granted me instant credibility, allowing me to speak at various networking events and hypnosis conferences. Being the person speaking in front of a room automatically positioned me as an expert, which significantly boosted my professional profile.

One of the most significant opportunities came from LinkedIn, where I was noticed by William Mitchell, an event organiser. He invited me to speak at the Heartland Hypnosis Conference in Missouri, USA. This was a game changer. Speaking overseas not only expanded my audience but also cemented my reputation as a global hypnotherapy leader.

At every presentation, I would give away copies of my book, and I had a table where attendees could purchase additional copies. This strategy not only increased my book sales but also enhanced my credibility and trustworthiness.

Expanding horizons: online programs and workshops

Realising that my growing international audience needed more than face-to-face retreats, I created an online program titled *The 15 Steps to Hypnosis Business Success*. This course, launched in April 2015, was a huge success, providing me with substantial passive income for many years.

My international presence continued to grow as I received invitations to speak at conferences in Boston, Las Vegas, New York, Chicago and London. I was even invited to be the keynote speaker at conferences in Missouri, Chicago, and New Zealand. These opportunities allowed me to create workshops and retreats in the USA, New Zealand and Australia, further solidifying my global influence.

Awards and recognition

In 2018, my efforts were recognised when I was awarded *Hypnotist of the Year* by the Mid America Conference in Chicago. This acknowledgment from my peers was a profound moment. When I asked the event organiser Carm why I was chosen, he simply said, 'Because your efforts do not go unnoticed'. Hearing this statement instantly brought tears to my eyes and a lump in my throat, as it reminded me of the countless hours I had felt alone and overwhelmed by the seemingly enormous responsibilities. Soon after, I also received an Outstanding Contribution Award from the International Certification Board of Clinical Hypnotherapy (ICBCH).

Building the HypnoFit® empire

My journey didn't stop at personal accolades. I went on to create the world's first global hypnotherapy network, with 22 locations across the USA, Canada, UK, New Zealand and Australia. My certified HypnoFit® trainers and myself trained 4,500 practitioners in the HypnoFit® Success System, ensuring a legacy of excellence and innovation in hypnotherapy.

The flagship clinic in Melbourne, which started with me seeing clients in my lounge room, is now a fully operational clinic with eight hypnotherapists and a clinic manager. This growth exemplifies how determination and strategic action can transform a small business into a global enterprise.

The legacy continues

I also developed a membership program called *Absolutely Everything Hypnosis,* featuring over 800 instructional videos. This program has a unique search key feature that allows users to find videos answering specific questions, providing a valuable resource for both new and experienced hypnotherapists.

The lifestyle benefits of building a successful hypnotherapy business

Today, I am semi-retired and live with my beloved fiancé Christian in a beautiful apartment overlooking the ocean. My income is entirely passive, a testament to the systems and structures I have built over the years.

Building a successful hypnotherapy business has not only transformed my professional life but also brought profound lifestyle benefits that I could have only dreamed of. The journey of creating a seven-figure business has provided me with the freedom, flexibility and financial security to live life on my own terms. Here are some of the remarkable ways my business success has enriched my life:

Financial freedom and security: One of the most significant lifestyle benefits has been the ability to achieve financial freedom and security. The success of my hypnotherapy business allowed me to pay off my son's home loan, giving him a solid financial foundation and peace of mind. Being able to support my family in such a substantial way has been incredibly fulfilling.

Maintaining stability through personal changes: Life is full of unexpected changes, and financial stability can provide a cushion during challenging times. When my husband and I decided to separate, I was able to pay him off and keep our house which was also where my business was located. This was a pivotal moment, as it allowed me to maintain a sense of stability and continuity in my life during a period of significant personal change.

The freedom to travel: With the financial success of my business, I gained the freedom to travel wherever and whenever I wanted. Even though I moved to Adelaide, I visit my family and my team back in Melbourne every month. Travel has always been a passion of mine, and being able to explore new destinations without financial constraints has been incredibly liberating. Whether it's a spontaneous weekend getaway or an extended overseas adventure, the ability to travel has enriched my life with new experiences, cultures, and perspectives. As I am writing this, I am looking forward to travelling to Melbourne, the Gold Coast, Hamilton Island, Hepburn Springs and Africa in the next six months.

Continuous personal and professional growth: Investing in my growth has always been a priority, and the financial success of my business has allowed me to continue doing so. I have been able to attend various courses, workshops and retreats, continuously expanding my knowledge and skills, and facilitating my newfound passion for spiritual growth.

Living off passive income: One of the most liberating aspects of my success has been the ability to completely stop all business activities, for a few years, and live off my passive income. This shift has provided me with the ultimate freedom to focus on what truly matters to me without the pressures of running a business. I now have the time to pursue my passions, spend quality time with my loved ones, and enjoy the simple pleasures of life.

Generosity towards family and team: Success has also enabled me to be generous with my family and my team. Being able to spoil my family, and share in their joys, has been immensely rewarding. Additionally, I have been able to show my appreciation for my dedicated team by offering them financial incentives, opportunities for growth, and a supportive work environment. Their hard work and loyalty have been instrumental in my success, and I am grateful to be in a position where I can give back to them.

Embracing a balanced lifestyle: With financial stability and the freedom to design my own schedule, I have embraced a balanced lifestyle that prioritises wellbeing and joy. I have more time to engage in activities that nourish my mind, body and soul. From meditation to spending time in nature and enjoying hobbies, my balanced lifestyle has brought a sense of peace and fulfillment that permeates every aspect of my life.

The power of generosity: Generosity has been a guiding principle throughout my journey. The ability to give freely, whether it's supporting the homeless, donating to a cause, or providing bonuses and gifts to my team, has brought immense joy and satisfaction. Generosity creates a ripple effect, fostering a culture of kindness and support that benefits everyone involved. It reinforces the values of compassion and integrity that are central to my life and business.

Lessons learned

Throughout my journey, I have learned invaluable lessons about perseverance, vision and the power of taking inspired action. These lessons have been the foundation of my success and have guided me through the ups and downs of building a global hypnotherapy network. Here are some key messages that I hope will inspire you:

1. **Dream big, start small:** My journey from seeing clients in my lounge room to creating a global network began with a single step. Don't be afraid to start small, but always keep your larger vision in mind. Every significant achievement starts with a humble beginning. By focusing on incremental progress and not being discouraged by the initial size of your endeavours, you lay a solid foundation for future growth.

2. **Take inspired action:** Success doesn't come to those who wait; it comes to those who take decisive, consistent action. Be proactive and seize opportunities as they arise. Inspired action is about aligning your efforts with your vision and taking steps that feel right to you. It's not just about working hard; it's about working smart and staying aligned with your goals.
3. **Invest in yourself:** Whether it's writing a book, attending workshops or seeking mentorship, investing in your personal and professional growth is crucial. This investment will pay off in ways you can't even imagine. Personal development is a lifelong journey. The knowledge and skills you acquire along the way will empower you to overcome obstacles and seize opportunities.
4. **Stay true to your vision:** There will be challenges and setbacks, but staying true to your vision will guide you through the tough times. Remember why you started and let that drive you forward. Your vision is your North Star. When times get tough, revisiting your original purpose and passion can reignite your motivation and help you stay on course.
5. **Leverage your success:** Use every achievement as a stepping stone to the next level. Whether it's a book, a speaking engagement or an award, leverage your successes to create even more opportunities. Success breeds success. Each accomplishment provides you with credibility and a platform to build upon. Don't be afraid to showcase your achievements and use them to open new doors.
6. **Build a strong network:** Surround yourself with people who support and inspire you. Your network can open doors and provide the encouragement you need to keep going. Relationships are the bedrock of any successful endeavour. By building a network of like-minded

individuals, mentors, and supporters, you create a support system that can help you navigate challenges and celebrate victories.
7. **Embrace change:** The journey to success is rarely a straight path. Embrace change and be flexible enough to adapt to new circumstances. Change can be daunting, but it also brings new opportunities. By staying open to change and being willing to pivot, when necessary, you can stay ahead of the curve and continually evolve.
8. **Cultivate resilience:** The ability to bounce back from setbacks is crucial. Cultivate resilience by learning from failures and viewing them as opportunities for growth. Resilience is a key trait of successful individuals. It's not about avoiding failure but about how you respond to it. Each setback is a learning experience that brings you closer to your goals.
9. **Focus on value:** Provide value in everything you do. Whether it's through your services, products or interactions, aim to make a positive impact. Focusing on value ensures that your work is meaningful and resonates with others. This not only enhances your reputation but also fosters lasting relationships with clients and peers.
10. **Relationships first:** Always remember the purpose behind your efforts. If you don't cherish and prioritise your relationships, all your hard work will be in vain.

The journey from my lounge room to becoming a global hypnotherapy leader has been filled with challenges, triumphs and invaluable lessons. Writing *Mindset Dominance* was a pivotal moment that set the stage for my success. It granted me credibility, opened doors and allowed me to share my message with a global audience.

As you pursue your own dreams, remember that anything is possible with the right mindset, determination and a willingness to take bold action. Let my journey inspire you to break free from self-sabotage, embrace your potential, and create a life of abundance and impact. Your dreams are within reach; all you need is the courage to take the first step and the perseverance to keep moving forward. The path to success is not always easy, but it is always worth it. Embrace your journey, learn from every experience, and never stop believing in your ability to connect to your inner greatness. It's ready and waiting for you.

With all my love,

Eleni (previously known as Helen Mitas)

CHAPTER 46

RACHAEL EVANS: MILLION DOLLAR MANIFESTOS – TURNING WORDS INTO WEALTH

Unveiling the hidden potential of book authorship

Welcome to the wild world of entrepreneurship, where the unexpected can often lead to the most rewarding journeys! If you told me years ago that part of me becoming a multimillion-dollar business owner would include being a thrice published author, I'd probably laugh and ask what you were smoking. But here we are, and it all started with one little book. Not just any book, but one that I never planned to write. This chapter is all about how the unexpected twists of book authorship can turn your business dreams into reality and, yes, how book sales alone won't make you rich – but they sure can open the right doors.

The accidental author: my first foray into writing

Picture this: it's early 2015, and I'm gearing up to exhibit at the Australian Automotive Aftermarket Expo. I'm thinking, how can I get these automotive technicians who are also small business owners – my ideal clients – to stop and actually talk to me? Then a peer suggests, 'Why not write a book?' A book? Really? But I took the plunge. Enter *Turbo Charged*, my first book. After a whirlwind weekend with the Ultimate 48 Hour Author team, I had a book in my hands and a whole new strategy in my head. The book wasn't about getting rich off sales – it was a lead magnet, pure and simple. And boy, did it attract!

The real genius behind *Turbo Charged* was its ability to act as a business card on steroids. It was something tangible that potential clients could hold, flip through, and connect with. It wasn't just my words they were reading; it was my expertise, my solutions to their problems, and a sneak peek into what working with me could look like. This was the magic formula that turned a simple book into a powerful business tool.

Building a strategy around books: the secret sauce

The books I've authored – *Turbo Charged*, *Poor to Profit* and *4-Day Work Week by Workshop Whisperer* – are more than just pretty covers and good reads. They're strategic tools designed to grab

PART 4: MILLIONAIRE AUTHORS

the attention of my niche audience: auto repair shop owners. Think of them as a golden handshake that gets potential clients into our world. By offering these books at low cost or as free downloads, we've drawn thousands of potential clients into our ecosystem. Each book is a stepping stone, a little nugget of wisdom that says, 'Hey, we know our stuff, and we can help you turn your business around.'

The creation process of these books was also a strategic endeavour. Each book was meticulously planned to address specific pain points within the industry. For example, *Poor to Profit* focused on transforming struggling businesses into profitable ventures, while *4-Day Work Week by Workshop Whisperer* introduced the revolutionary concept of optimising business operations to achieve a balanced lifestyle. By tailoring the content to meet the exact needs of our audience, we ensured that each book resonated deeply, establishing us as trusted experts.

Tactical use of books as lead magnets: the master plan

Here's where it gets juicy. We didn't just write books and hope for the best. We deployed them like strategic missiles. Targeted email campaigns, Facebook ads, you name it. We funnelled potential clients to landing pages where they could download our books in exchange for their contact info. This method not only built our mailing list but also established trust. People don't just buy books – they buy into the author's expertise. And once they're in,

we nurture that relationship with educational emails, guiding them gently but firmly towards becoming paying clients. It's all about playing the long game.

Our email campaigns were designed to provide ongoing value. Each email wasn't just a sales pitch; it was a mini masterclass packed with actionable tips and insights. This approach kept our audience engaged and eager for more, slowly building a foundation of trust and authority. Over time, this steady stream of valuable content transformed casual readers into loyal clients who were ready to invest in our higher-ticket coaching programs.

From leads to long-term success: the tale of Chris

Let's talk about Chris. Chris is a shining example of how this strategy works. He stumbled upon *Turbo Charged* through an early download. His business was okay but stuck in a rut. After diving into our coaching program – sparked by the insights from the book – we identified operational bottlenecks and growth opportunities. By empowering his team and optimising processes, Chris turned his business into a multi-seven-figure powerhouse, running on a four-day work week. And it all started with a book download. How amazing is that?!

Chris's story is a testament to the transformative power of our approach. When Chris first engaged with us, he was overwhelmed, working long hours, and struggling to see significant growth. Through our coaching, we helped him implement effective systems and processes that streamlined his operations. This not only boosted his business efficiency but also improved his quality of life. Today, Chris enjoys the freedom to spend more time with his family, all while his business continues to thrive. His success is a shining example of what's possible when you combine insightful content with strategic coaching.

Financial intelligence: turning coaching profits into investments

Here's the kicker: the money we made from coaching wasn't just for spending – it was for growing. My husband Dean and I knew we had to be smart about our profits. We learned about financial prudence, cash management and investment strategies. We didn't just keep the money in the business; we diversified into property and shares. The right advisors and a solid cash management system were game changers. Our investments outside the business are now worth four times what the business itself is worth. Talk about a return on investment!

Our approach to financial intelligence wasn't just about making money – it was about making smart money. We focused on understanding the financial landscape and making informed decisions that would ensure long-term stability and growth. This included setting up a self-managed super fund, investing in high-growth properties, and diversifying our portfolio with shares. The key was to create multiple streams of income that would continue to generate wealth, even when the business wasn't actively producing revenue. This strategic diversification has been crucial in securing our financial future and achieving true financial independence.

Overcoming challenges: the realities of book marketing

It wasn't all smooth sailing. Getting potential clients to notice our books was a challenge. We had to invest time, money and brainpower into marketing strategies that would resonate with our audience. But persistence paid off. We tested, learned, adapted and eventually cracked the code. Our books started reaching the right people, making the right impact. And once they were in, the nurturing process began, transforming prospects into loyal clients.

One of the biggest challenges we faced was the noise in the general business coaching market. With so many voices vying for attention, standing out required creativity and persistence. My book, being industry specific and not like so many generalist business books, required some creativity. We experimented with different marketing tactics, from social media ads to old school industry magazines in print, to ensure our books reached the right audience. We also leveraged our network, collaborating with other industry leaders to promote our books and extend our reach. These efforts paid off, gradually building a strong presence and attracting a steady stream of leads.

Evolution of strategy: always be adapting

The strategy evolved over time. We realised that books were not just for visibility and client acquisition but also gateways to deeper engagements. They became conversation starters, allowing us to build a narrative with potential clients that extended beyond the initial read. We used books to offer a glimpse into the transformative potential of our coaching programs. This shift in strategy ensured that our methods stayed fresh and effective, keeping us ahead in a competitive market.

As the market evolved, so did our approach. We continuously monitored trends and adapted our strategies to stay relevant. This included updating our books with new content, launching digital versions, and even creating companion guides and workbooks to enhance the reader's experience. By staying agile and responsive to market changes, we maintained our competitive edge and continued to attract and engage our target audience.

The long-term impact: more than just business

Being a published author has done wonders for my professional credibility and opened doors I never imagined. High-value speaking engagements, international recognition, and collaborations all flowed from the authority established through my books. But beyond the professional gains, the personal satisfaction of helping thousands of business owners turn their dreams into reality has been incredibly rewarding. Seeing others succeed because of the knowledge I've shared is the ultimate high.

The ripple effects of authorship have extended into every facet of my life. Each book has not only boosted my business but also enriched my personal journey. The connections made, the lives touched and the stories shared have all contributed to a fulfilling and purposeful career. Moreover, the pride my family feels, especially my kids seeing their mum as a published author, adds a special layer of joy and accomplishment to this journey.

Mastering the art of the million-dollar manifesto

Looking back, writing *Turbo Charged* was a game changer. Each book since has built on that foundation, amplifying my reputation and expanding my influence. As I continue to share my expertise, the strategies from my early days of book authorship remain central – turning knowledge into wealth, one page at a time. So, here's the deal: don't think of your book as the end goal. Think of it as the beginning of something much bigger. Write, share and leverage your knowledge to build connections, trust, and ultimately, wealth. It's not just about the sales – it's about the journey those sales can start.

CHAPTER 47

FRANCESCA MOI – DELEGATE AND DOMINATE

Hello, My name is Francesca Moi, and I'm the founder of Empowering Virtual Solution.

About eight years ago, I had the incredible opportunity to meet Natasa Denman from Ultimate 48 Hour Author. During our conversation, Natasa encouraged me, 'You should write a book.' At that time, my business was in its early stages, generating around $120,000 annually. I was gaining some momentum, but I still questioned myself: 'Who am I to write a book? I'm not yet running a million-dollar business. Am I truly ready to write a book? Do I have enough expertise?' Despite these doubts, I was intrigued by Natasa description of a book as a 'business card on steroids', and I decided to take the plunge.

Natasa always says it's not just about the book you write, but who you become when you hold that book in your hands. That really hit home for me. Writing that book didn't just turn me into an author – it gave me a whole new level of confidence. Suddenly, I wasn't just someone struggling to get a business off the ground; I was a published author.

That shift changed how people saw me, too. I could feel the difference in their reactions; it was like they took me more seriously, and that boosted my confidence even more. But let's be clear – the book alone didn't catapult my business to a million dollars in three and a half years. That part required serious investments. I poured money into coaching and mentoring to understand exactly what it would take to scale my business from $120,000 to $1.5 million. I had to strategise and implement a variety of new approaches to really take my business to another level.

When my financial situation improved enough to start hiring staff, it was a game changer. I no longer had to shoulder everything myself. A lot of people think publishing a book will solve all their business problems. They expect the book to do all the heavy lifting. That wasn't the case for me. In fact, I didn't sell many copies at first – just about a hundred. Now, we print around 500 copies each year, but we mostly give them away as a powerful networking tool, just like Natasa suggested, as a 'business card on steroids'.

It's a way for us to introduce ourselves – 'Hey, take a look at what I do, get to know my work.' And you know what? It works. People read it, share it, and then I get calls saying, 'Hey, someone passed me your book, and I'd love to work with you.'

The book has been a game changer in ways that go beyond direct sales. It's not just about the copies sold, it's how the book has opened doors for me. Reaching the $1.5 million mark in our business was a huge milestone, and from there, I decided to diversify our investments. I even used one of our properties as a dual-purpose space – by day, it serves as our office, and by night, we list it on Airbnb. This setup not only maximises our investment but also keeps things interesting around here.

We've also expanded our team, bringing on eight full-time staff members in the Philippines. Their main job? To help market the book and our services. They work hard to get our name out there, helping build a trusting relationship with our audience. You see, it's said that people need about 11 hours of engaging with a brand before they feel confident enough to buy. Our book might cover about four to five hours of that, so we needed to find additional ways to fill in the rest. That's where our active social media presence comes into play.

I personally don't manage our social media – that's where our fantastic virtual assistants shine. They take the videos I record, transcribe them, and turn them into engaging posts and content online. This strategy is vital because it maintains our visibility and helps us connect with our audience on a deeper level.

It's really a shame that so many people put their heart and soul into writing a book, only to stop there. They miss out on the opportunity to use their book as a springboard to enhance their business. We've focused on integrating the book into a broader business strategy, which has been essential for our growth and continued success.

The book, to me, feels like the backbone of our business strategy. I am currently working on my fourth book, titled *The Power of Delegation*. It's all about helping business owners understand why and how they should delegate tasks to a virtual assistant.

In the 12 chapters of the book, we dive deep, but the main takeaway is simple: if you're a business owner, you don't have time to find talent and manage everything yourself. My book cuts straight to the point – it shows that I know what I'm talking about. So, instead of you struggling on your own, why not let me and my team find the right people for you? It's like a shortcut to success.

I see each book as a stepping stone, an entry point to connect with people who need our help. With this fourth book, I've taken things a step further. I created a business model that leverages the book to propel us to new heights. You can either build a business around a book, or, like I did this time, use the book to elevate an existing business.

So here's what my marketing plan with my fourth book is: I'm going to hit up co-working spaces and really connect with the managers and founders there. I'll offer a free book to everyone who joins the space, and even to those who are already members. It's a great way for us to build trust with an audience that's already right there, and it lets us get our message in front of them more directly and quickly.

I like to think of the book as a supercharged business card. Imagine walking into a co-working space, being handed a free book with a friendly, 'Congratulations! If you haven't started delegating yet, this book will show you how.' It's a straightforward and effective way to start a conversation.

Building a business around a book, or using a book to boost your existing business, is incredibly powerful. It's not just about the content of the book, it's about using the book as a tool to take your business to a whole new level.

And here's the thing – I'm the biggest investor in my business. I've taken many risks and invested heavily because I believe that the more you put in, the more you get out. I've spent a lot on training for myself and my team, on coaches, on various learning programs. All this investment is why I can now afford to work only about 20 hours a week. It allows me to take time off, travel and pursue my passions – like when I was a full-time chef for five years. Right now, I'm focusing on a different direction in my health journey, but the flexibility I have is incredible.

It's important to remember that success like this doesn't happen overnight. You don't just publish a book and watch your business explode. It's about consistently putting yourself and your business out there. That's how you make it happen.

I often tell people that my book wouldn't have made much impact if I didn't already have an audience. It's like putting up a billboard in the middle of a desert; if there's no-one around to see it, what's the point? There's really no use in having a book or a website about it if there's no audience to engage with it.

That's exactly why I've poured so much effort into building a solid social media presence. I've worked tirelessly to create a community around my brand because without that visibility on social media, I wouldn't have been able to grow my business the way I have.

I managed to build not just one, but two businesses that each surpassed the $1 million mark. The first took about three and a half years to build, while the second only took 14 months. By then, I had a clear idea of what worked and what didn't, which strategies to leverage, and how to scale quickly. This time, I chose to integrate the book once the business had already reached the million-dollar threshold. I might have introduced it earlier, but everything needed to be just right – I needed that solid foundation first.

Now, as I aim to forge stronger connections with larger corporations, the book is more than just a publication; it's a strategic tool, a shortcut to building relationships. It helps open doors and start conversations that might have otherwise taken much longer to initiate.

Another thing I love doing with my book is bringing it along to events. I picked up this tip from Natasa. At these events, I sometimes offer it as a prize or just hand it out to people I chat with. It's such a thrill to see their reactions, like, 'Oh my gosh, you're giving me your book? Thank you, please sign it!' It instantly boosts my credibility and gets people to take me and my business more seriously.

The book and the business really go hand in hand. It's not about one building the other – they complement each other, helping to construct an empire over time.

If I were to give one piece of advice to someone just starting out with their book, it would be to stay consistent. Consistency drives momentum, and momentum is what builds a successful business.

If you find you don't have the time or patience to consistently update your social media or to build relationships, consider outsourcing these tasks. That's exactly why we set up our virtual assistant business. We've done it successfully for ourselves, building two businesses with the help of virtual assistants, and now we want to help others do the same. It really is a secret to success.

Ultimately, your book can be a powerful tool for your business. You can use it to generate content for social media, create a series of videos discussing its themes, and much more. While the book alone won't guarantee success, it's a crucial step that supports your credibility and enhances your visibility. It's not just a milestone – it's a stepping stone to greater achievements in your business journey.

I'm thrilled that I've written four books so far, all with the incredible support of Natasa, Stuart and the whole team. I'm particularly excited about my fourth book, which is just about to be released. I'm already committed to continuing this journey, planning to write more because I've seen firsthand how much credibility they add. In fact, I've just landed a speaking gig with a major corporation thanks to my book, *Invisible to Invincible*.

Back in 2015, that same book opened up another fantastic opportunity. Someone passed it along within their corporate network, which led them to invite me to speak about social media at their conference – a paid gig. This just shows that even my earlier books continue to bring in business opportunities because I keep my social media presence active and engaging. If someone picks up my book and then checks out my social media only to find it outdated, they might think I'm no longer active in my field. So, staying visible online is crucial. It really helps in building wealth.

PART 4: MILLIONAIRE AUTHORS

My lifestyle now is incredible because I can leverage my work effectively. Having rich content in my books allows my virtual assistants to independently manage our social media content without needing my constant input. I love how efficient Natasa's strategy has made the writing process. We managed to finish this latest book in just about a month and a half by knocking out two chapters a week for six weeks. Seeing the positive impact these books have had, not just on my business but also on my personal life, is truly rewarding.

CHAPTER 48

I had to finish off on Chapter 48 – after all I am the Ultimate 48 Hour Author, however this resource is not in the book. I invite you to continue your journey to becoming a millionaire author by accessing the 80-Point First Time Author Checklist here: http://bit.ly/checklist80

ABOUT THE AUTHOR

Natasa Denman was born in Skopje, Macedonia and immigrated to Melbourne, Australia at the age of 14. Her mum left her behind (not in a bad way) when she was 11 and a half to try to set up a life in Australia. Although she didn't speak any English yet, she completed her schooling successfully. She has a Bachelor of Applied Science (Psychology/Psychophysiology), Diploma in IT and Diploma in Life Coaching. Natasa is also an NLP Practitioner and has a Black Belt in Taekwondo.

After 12 years in the optical industry a life-altering event shifted Natasa's focus to personal development and starting her business in May 2010. Her first book *The 7 Ultimate Secrets to Weight Loss* was the defining moment in building her credibility and clientele into a viable and profitable business.

In 2013, Natasa launched her now famous brand Ultimate 48 Hour Author and at the time of writing this has completed 50 Ultimate 48 Hour Author retreats and has helped over 1000 authors write more than 1300 books. The business pivoted fully online in March 2020 and thrived during the pandemic.

Natasa is married to Stuart Denman and they have three amazing children in Judd, Mika and Xara. They work hard as a team together in the business and travel four months out of every year building on memories and experiences with their loved ones.

Email: natasa@natasadenman.com
Websites: www.writeabook.com.au and www.natasadenman.com

Come along to our Signature FREE Event Online or in Person – check out options and next dates on our website.

Read or watch reviews here:
Google - https://bit.ly/googlereviews48
LinkedIn - https://bit.ly/linkedinnatasadenman
Facebook Fan page - https://bit.ly/facebookfan48
You Tube - https://bit.ly/youtubenatasadenman
Author Interviews: https://bit.ly/authorinterviews48

THE DENMAN FAMILY COLLECTION OF BOOKS

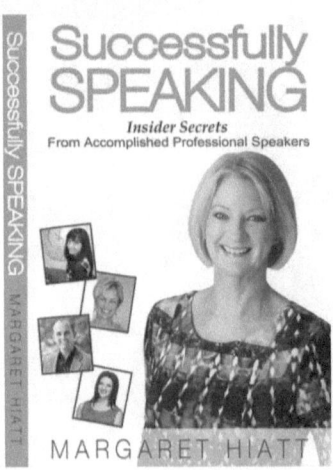

THE DENMAN FAMILY COLLECTION OF BOOKS

Buy anyone of these titles at
https://www.writeabook.com.au/shop/

www.ingramcontent.com/pod-product-compliance
Lightning Source LLC
Chambersburg PA
CBHW030039100526
44590CB00011B/265